PRAISE FOR *Script & Scribble*

"This is a book every writer would love, a curio cabinet on the art and act of writing."   —Amy Tan, author of *Saving Fish from Drowning*

"A winsome mix of memoir and call to arms . . . An entertaining history."   —*Chicago Tribune*, Editor's Choice

"A witty and readable (and fetchingly illustrated and glossed) excursion through the history of handwriting."   —Cullen Murphy, *The Wall Street Journal*

"Highly enjoyable . . . Witty and often endearingly autobiographical."
—Michael Dirda, *The Washington Post*

"A charming, illustrated eulogy to a craft that's fast losing its place in the modern world."   —*Financial Times*

"Florey's argument is nostalgic yet pragmatic. 'It seems wrong,' she says, 'when something beautiful, useful, and historically important vanishes.' Charmingly composed and handsomely presented, *Script and Scribble* just might provoke a handwriting revival."
—*The Boston Globe*

"[A] pithy account of the history of handwriting . . . Florey makes a solid case for handwriting as a social indicator, and her affection for its art is thoughtful and aesthetically informed." —Albert Mobilio, *Bookforum*

"Kitty Burns Florey's charming history of the rise and fall of handwriting is a loving and polished tribute to a modest but deeply civilizing skill that can make our words not only intelligible to others but, like this book, sweet and beautiful."   —David Skinner, author of *The Story of Ain't: America, Its Language, and the Most Controversial Dictionary Ever Published*

"Florey . . . lovingly traces the history of handwriting, from its ancient birth to its imminent demise."   —Sam Anderson, *New York*

"What in God's name has happened to penmanship? It's easy to blame the computer, but, as Kitty Burns Florey demonstrates in her thoughtful, witty, and sensible book, the story goes far deeper than that. It touches on the way we think, the way we write, and the way we lead our lives. Read *Script & Scribble* and be enlightened."
—Ben Yagoda, author of *When You Catch an Adjective, Kill It: The Parts of Speech, for Better And/Or Worse*

"Part memoir, part meticulously researched primer, [this] captivating history of handwriting is a lovely ode to a nearly lost art."
—*ReadyMade*

"Frank and engaging."   —*Rain Taxi*

Script and Scribble
The Rise and Fall of Handwriting

KITTY BURNS FLOREY

MELVILLE HOUSE
BROOKLYN · LONDON

FIRST MELVILLE HOUSE PRINTING OF
THE PAPERBACK EDITION: SEPTEMBER 2013

BOOK DESIGN: CAROL HAYES

MELVILLE HOUSE PUBLISHING   8 BLACKSTOCK MEWS
145 PLYMOUTH STREET   AND   ISLINGTON
BROOKLYN, NY 11201   LONDON N4 2BT

MHPBOOKS.COM   FACEBOOK.COM/MHPBOOKS   @MELVILLEHOUSE

ISBN: 978-1-61219-304-5

PRINTED IN THE UNITED STATES OF AMERICA
1 3 5 7 9 10 8 6 4 2

THE LIBRARY OF CONGRESS HAS CATALOGED
THE HARDCOVER EDITION OF THIS BOOK AS FOLLOWS:

FLOREY, KITTY BURNS.
SCRIPT AND SCRIBBLE : THE RISE AND FALL OF HANDWRITING / KITTY BURNS FLOREY.
P. CM.
ISBN 978-1-933633-67-1
1. PENMANSHIP. 2. PENMANSHIP, AMERICAN—HISTORY
3. WRITING—MATERIALS AND INSTRUMENTS—HISTORY.
4. GRAPHOLOGY. I. TITLE.
Z43.F58 2008
652'.1—DC22
2008026964

For Eileen and Rosamond

TABLE OF CONTENTS

*A true source of human happiness
lies in taking a genuine
interest in all the details of daily life
and elevating them by art.*

WILLIAM MORRIS

A Handwritten Life

Since I first picked up a pen, I have been under the spell of handwriting. I've experimented endlessly with different scripts: straight up, right-slanting, left-slanting, print-like, florid, spare, minimalist, maximalist, round, spiky, highly legible, insouciantly scrawled. I can't make a list or write a check without scrutinizing my rushed, ugly *F*'s and illegible *r*'s and wishing I'd taken more time or had a better artistic sense. When I doodle, I often doodle handwriting styles.

I suspect that, for many, this preoccupation might seem bizarre, even slightly mad. There's a widespread belief that, in a digital world, forming letters on paper with a pen is pointless and obsolete, and that anyone who thinks otherwise is right up there with folks who still have fallout shelters in their back yards. But I'm part of the last generation for whom handwriting was taught as a vital skill. All through school, it was an important part of our lives: you had good handwriting, or you had bad handwriting—at some level, the way you wrote was a part of you, and was judged. That identification with my own script has never left me.

Recent doodle retrieved from wastebasket

When I look back at learning to write, I can still feel the excitement of it. Little kids printed. Big kids wrote in longhand.

I learned to write longhand—cursive—in third grade at St. John the Baptist Academy in Syracuse, New York. Above the blackboard there was a frieze showing the idealized script we were all aiming at, in both upper and lower case, and lurking in each student's beat-up old wooden desk was a Palmer Method workbook.

Every day, during handwriting practice, we took out our workbooks, sat up straight at our desks, and grabbed our pencils. Sister Victorine swished around the room in her long black habit, looking over our shoulders with her eagle eye and beating time like an orchestra conductor—*one two, one two, up down, up down*—a brisk martial rhythm that we labored to match with the strokes of our pencils.[1]

1 A friend of mine remembers doing this more romantically to the strains of "The Blue Danube."

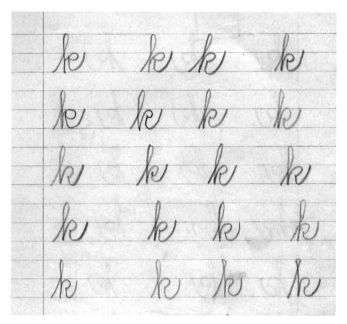

From Sister Victorine's class

Form, size, slant, spacing: those were the elements of the Palmer Method. At the end of the session, if you managed to keep them all in mind while you sat straight but also stayed relaxed, and if you concentrated on what you were doing instead of wishing you were out in the school yard playing Red Rover, you had pages of perfect ovals, upstrokes, and downstrokes, and by the end of third grade, these would have come together into some species of legible penmanship.

Sister Victorine was a tall, stately nun with mild blue eyes, round gun-metal glasses, and a black thumbnail on her right hand. The black thumb mesmerized me. I asked my parents where you got such a thing. My father said, "Maybe she hit her thumb with a hammer." My mother winced absently and said, "Oh dear." They clearly weren't as compelled by it as I was. While I watched Sister Victorine write flawless cursive homilies on the blackboard—*Pride goes before a fall, Haste makes waste*—I pictured her lifting the hammer to pound a nail, whacking her thumb instead, the thumb turning a rich black as she looked at it in horror. What made it turn black? And why would a nun have been pounding a nail? Did she cry? Did nuns cry? Or had it happened before she even entered the convent? I imagined a tough and gritty childhood, forced labor in her cruel father's carpentry shop. Was that why she became a nun? To escape?

With difficulty, I would turn my attention from her fascinating thumbnail and work at copying her flowing capital *L*'s and trimly crossed *t*'s. I wasn't a superstar, but I was pretty good at it, and I didn't mind handwriting practice. Something about the low-key creativity, the reach for perfection, and the repetitive mental numbness of it appealed to me—still does.

By the time we left Sister Victorine and entered Sister Robert Clare's fourth-grade class, we were deemed to be accomplished hand-writers and were allowed to progress from pencils

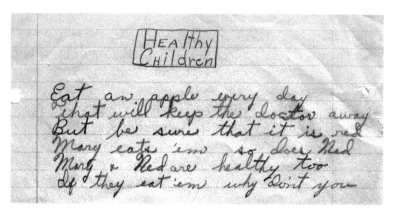

Third grade

to straight pens, which cost a nickel each. They were fitted
with metal points (nibs) that we dipped into small glass
inkwells that sat in a hole at the upper right (too bad, lefties!)
corner of our desks. Writing with a straight pen dunked into
an inkwell was an adventure: the path from ink to paper could
be a sea of blots and blobs, and keeping the ink-flow steady on
the paper was maddeningly difficult.

2 In third and fourth
grades, my ambition
was to become a
famous poet. This has
not happened.

Fourth grade[2]

By fifth grade, we had graduated to fountain pens[3] and were writing with some fluency—well enough, at least, to stop worrying about getting it right and start thinking about what impression we were making. This was the age when pen obsessives were born. In the diary I kept when I was ten, one of my New Year's resolutions was: "I will write ROUND"—ROUND was a fad among my set—and so I did:

Patently insincere school assignment, fifth grade

It wasn't until high school that the nuns finally allowed us, grudgingly, to write with ball-points. In my school, at least, there was a nunly prejudice against them as newfangled nonsense: the ball-points of the day were regarded as not only unreliable and messy (they did tend to skip and smear) but extravagant: when the ink ran out, you threw away the innards and bought a refill! It was almost as bad as buying a new pen every time! But among us devil-may-care adolescents, who worried about such trivial concerns? I was very fond of my blue Esterbrook fountain pen, my collaborator in hours of scriptomaniacal experiments. But everyone knew that ball-point pens were way cool, and eventually the nuns stopped fighting them.

3 We had also begun to acquire a curious artifact of the Pre-Computer Era (PCE), the "writer's bump"—a callous at the place where the thumb and first two fingers come together (known as the "dynamic tripod" in serious handwriting circles) to hold the pen. The bump forms at the top joint of the middle finger. There was a time when everyone had one, and it grew in size until, by the time you were in your teens, it was a prominent lump. It wasn't considered unsightly or even worthy of notice. It was a fact of life, like a nose. I still have the vestige of mine.

> men. It is, perhaps, true that Poe wrote with little variation, his themes being for the most part, a morbid, excessively sad, haunting preoccupation with death. But Poe fulfilled his avowed function — that of creating beauty — admirably & originally. His poetry exemplifies the fascination of the bizarre & his language, images, &

Discuss

Smeared ballpoint, twelfth grade

Then felt tips came along. I remember when the first benzene-scented Magic Markers hit my high school, first in basic black, soon in glorious Technicolor. If you handed me one now, its intoxicating chemical stink would, in a Proustian second, transport me back to a winter afternoon at St. John's when, wearing a hideous maroon serge uniform, knee socks, and saddle shoes, I sat with a group of fellow students and, with colorfully marker-stained hands, made signs for pep rallies: BEAT ASSUMPTION! CRUSH SACRED HEART!—sentiments comprehensible, perhaps, only to basketball-crazed parochial school students without a shred of irony.

I used to change my handwriting the way I changed my hair color (my natural mousy brown ran the gamut from a sort of palomino[4] to a daring reddish-black). It's obvious now that most of my scriptorial attempts were outrageously pretentious, appallingly twee, but I considered each one the height of cool—the proper handwriting for an aspiring Bohemian, a future writer, a deeply sensitive person who wrote deeply sensitive poetry and then burned it in the sink, weeping. Just as nineteenth-century ink nuts—a common species in those days—believed that good penmanship would lead directly to good moral character, I think I must have believed that an arty style would make me an artist.

4 When at age sixteen I discovered Marchand's Golden Hair Wash and came into school a streaky blonde, the nuns sent me straight home again.

What I was really looking for, of course, was my self. The notion that it would arrive through a bottle of Miss Clairol or the way I made a capital *B* was not, I hope, entirely inappropriate for my age group.

Over the years, I've become less flighty and self-conscious, and so has my handwriting. It gradually ceased its adventurous traveling, settling at last into a fitfully legible debased scribble that often looks, to me, not only plug-ugly but slightly berserk:

The tragedy of old age is not that one is old but that one is young.
Oscar Wilde

Where is the fluent Palmer Method succession of ovals and loops I learned in elementary school and took such pains to perfect? What happened to the drop-dead-arty script I cultivated in college as a symbol of emancipation from my lackluster and conventional past? Whither the briskly legible semi-cursive in which I wrote the rough drafts of my first few novels, at a time when keyboards existed only on typewriters and on the old piano everyone had in the corner of the living room?

The glory days of elegant handwriting have long been over. In our times, what is the practical use of good penmanship?[5] How often do most of us need to write with an actual pen on actual paper? Diana, princess of Wales, got into her secondary school on the strength of her neat handwriting. In Ha Jin's novel *Waiting*, set in his native China, a young woman is jilted by a suitor because her writing is unattractive. And aspiring

5 Or "penpersonship"— there are at least 200 very sincere Google references to this version, as in "It's essential to have good penpersonship."

bakers can still move up to cake decorating only if they can squeeze out a beautiful "Happy Birthday."

For most of us, it's less crucial—or so goes the conventional wisdom. We make shopping lists, we jot things down in meetings, we send an occasional thank-you letter, we address our Christmas cards, sometimes write a few lines inside. Students take notes in class and write test answers by hand. We scribble on the ubiquitous Post-its and stick them up on the borders of the computer screen.

But when it comes to our "real" writing, we are all, all slaves to the keyboard. A vast number of people work at one for most of the day. Others dash to the screen to check e-mail the minute they get home, or live in a continual round of IM-ing and text-messaging on a PDA or a mobile phone. Few teachers now find time or have the inclination to work handwriting instruction into the curriculum; keyboarding is being taught in its place. A stroll into any Starbucks will find a laptop propped in front of at least half the customers. I acquired my first computer in 1985, long before anyone else I knew had one. Less than a quarter-century later, the tapping of keys can be heard around the planet.

We live in a fast-moving stripped-down world, one that's often efficient to the point of sterility. There was a time when we went to the movies in gorgeously embellished theaters with Moorish tiles, grand staircases, brass-railed balconies, uniformed ushers with flashlights; now movies are shown in concrete multiplexes where the noise of the gun fight in shoebox 17 bleeds into the noise of the car chase in matchbox 18. Once, department stores were dazzling mezzanined emporia where the saleswomen wore dresses and high heels and the salesmen natty suits and ties.

Now we shop in airplane hangars with names like Kmart and Target and Wal-Mart.[6] Supermarkets are massive megastores where you can clock a mile just hunting for a can of

6 Where there are no salespeople at all, just bored and underpaid checkout clerks without health benefits.

Saleslady and customer, 1944

chickpeas. Banks are no longer soaring, Greek-columned temples to Mammon but drab ex-shoestores with plastic logos blasted across the front. People used to dress up for all kinds of things: church, shopping, dentist appointments, plane trips; now we dress mostly for comfort, and getting gussied up is only for very special occasions, like weddings, New Year's Eve, maybe opening night at the opera. Food is fast, service is slow, telephones are answered by robots.

This is not meant to be a boomer rant. I'm not saying any of this is bad. Some of it seems a huge improvement on the past (I wouldn't want to go shopping in high heels and nylons even if I owned any) and some of it doesn't (I wish some nice man in a cap would pump the gas for my Subaru, wash the windows, and give me a free road map, too). It's simply the world as we know it.

We no longer have to spend time lacing our corsets or sharpening our quills, but for many reasons we're all in a hurry, too busy to dress up, or make gooseberry jam, or dampen a shirt,[7] wrap it in a towel, and let it sit for an hour before ironing it (a domestic ritual I was brought up on and continued to observe

7 At our house, this was done with an old Heinz ketchup bottle fitted with the kind of sprinkler top that was readily available at any hardware store.

until I was in my thirties). I look back on some of these activities with astonishment. Did I really do chores on Saturday mornings that included polishing the bathroom faucets with Glass Wax? Did my mother really come home from work and sit down with her sewing? Did airline stewardesses really wobble down the aisle in spike heels and tight navy blue skirts?

And, as ironing and nylons go, so, apparently, goes penmanship.

* * * *

I've had a recurring dream since I was a kid—I'm looking at a piece of paper with words written on it in black ink. The writing is a clear, ordinary cursive script, but no matter how I try, I can't read it. When I was very young, the words were sometimes written in pencil in a book or sewn with black thread on a piece of white satin in an embroidery hoop. (Not so strange, maybe: in those days most females embroidered, including my grandmother, my mother, and me. But as time has gone by, it has refined itself to this enigmatic dream of pen, paper, ink, and incomprehensibility.)

I've begun to wonder if, in its most recent manifestations, the dream is the scary premonition of an ink nut who fears that the day is coming when no one will be able to read handwriting at all.

Chapter One

Pen, Paper, Ink—
A Stroll Through
Handwriting History

THE STYLUS, THE BRUSH, AND THE CALAMUS

The human need—or maybe the urge—to record the minutiae of daily life goes back to cave dwellers scratching on walls with sharp stones. That instinct, as the British calligrapher Donald Jackson puts it in *The Story of Writing* (1980), "is as deep-rooted as anything we know about our earliest ancestors." They began by making pictures that recorded the results of the hunt. Eventually, drawing a picture of each slain bison became cumbersome and time-consuming, and a simpler method was developed: the use of a symbol to stand for a thing.

In the fourth millennium BC, the Sumerians were drawing pictures on wet clay of the objects that made up their world—a tree, say, or a house. These were incised with a stylus, a pencil-like instrument not unlike the ones used with today's PDAs, and because its tip was triangular, the marks were wedge-shaped (hence, *cuneiform*, from the Latin *cuneus*, meaning *wedge*).

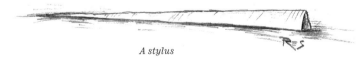

A stylus

These stylized images—pictograms—were used to record business transactions, historical events, and recipes, including one for beer, which the Sumerians apparently invented.[1] Over time, their symbols lost detail and became increasingly abstracted, a response to the roughness of the stylus as a writing tool, and tendency of the clay to harden rapidly. The pictograms began to give way to phonograms, in which an image represented the sound of a syllable rather than an object—a radical transformation that reduced the two thousand images of the Sumerians to two hundred.

At the same time, the Egyptians began chiseling their elegant hieroglyphs ("writing of the gods") into stone or painting them on papyrus, using either a brush made of bristles, or a brush-pen made by chewing or hammering one end of a reed until it was soft. The Egyptians actually had an alphabet of twenty-four letters (all consonants), but because of the relative flexibility of the brush on papyrus, the urgency that led the stylus-and-clay Sumerians toward simplification was absent. The Egyptians hung on to their pictograms long past the point where they were needed. Hieroglyphics were a composite of pictograms and phonograms, the two types of images often supplementing each other in a phenomenally complex system: a student of writing had to memorize hundreds of separate signs.

Over time, pictograms in general became less realistic and more abstract, until finally, sometime before the first millennium BC, the Phoenicians—the most successful traders and businessmen of their day—took a crucial leap further and devised the first system of writing dependent entirely on sounds rather than on images. A symbol now stood for a sound, not for a syllable. Their ingenious system of letters—a tidy twenty-six as opposed to hundreds—was worked out by merchants in the Phoenician city of Byblos—the city the Greeks had named after their word for *papyrus* because Egyptian papyrus was shipped from there. (*Byblos*, of course, is the source of bookish words like *bibliography* and *bible*.)

The Phoenician system was based, quite sensibly, on Egyptian hieroglyphics: the genius of the Phoenicians was to transform the pictograms into a true alphabet. The Egyptian sign for *ox head*, for example, was:

The Phoenician word for *ox* was *aleph*, and they named the letter by the initial sound of what the pictogram had represented (aleph = *A*) so that meaning was derived from a sound rather than from a picture. Similarly, the Egyptians used this expressive sign for *water:*

The Phoenicians called it *mem*, their word for *water,* and it became *M*. (If we called our letter *M* not *em* but, say, *Mom*, and our letter *A ax*, we might be learning not our *ABCs* but our *Ax-Banana-Cats*. This process is called acrophony, from the Greek words for "uppermost" and "sound.") Because they were still using a stylus, the letters began as angular forms, but eventually they also began to use brush and ink to generate more rounded letters. Gradually, a complete alphabet evolved and—with some modifications and additions over the slow flow of time—it's the alphabet we use today.

Between the Phoenicians with their inventories and bills of lading, and the monastic scribes toiling over illuminated manuscripts in their scriptoria, were the Romans. The Romans devised their own take on the Phoenician alphabet, using innovations borrowed from the Greeks and the Etruscans to create a bold, impressive all-caps script worthy of world conquerors. It became known as Roman Square Capital, and was particularly well suited to incising large letters with a chisel and mallet onto the stone facades of buildings.

SENATVS·POPVLVSQVE·RO IMP·CAESARI·DIVI·NERVAE· TRAIANOAVGGERM·DACIOP

Roman Square Capital

The Romans employed more casual scripts as well, designed to be scribbled rather than chiseled, including an early cursive for writing quickly if not beautifully: when Julius Caesar, on horseback, dictated letters in the midst of a military campaign (as Plutarch tells us he did), the scribes very likely jotted down his words in their messy, shorthand proto-cursive and copied them over neatly in Square Capital when they got back to their tents.

Much of this early writing (i.e., getting words onto a flat surface) was done using some version of the stylus on wax *tabulae*—shallow book-sized wooden or ivory boxes covered with a film of beeswax stained dark to make the writing more legible—an apparatus that calls to mind the once-ubiquitous Magic Slate.

Gradually, the instrument's wedge-shaped end became more pointed, but the other remained flat for smoothing out the wax in order to use the surface again (or to "erase" an error). The stylus could be plain as a knitting needle or turned

A woman with stylus and tabula, from Pompeii

like a spindle, and was usually made of iron or bone (or iron-tipped bone), sometimes of more expensive bronze.

Scholars estimate that perhaps 15 percent of Romans were literate, most of them from the patrician class. An educated citizen carried a stylus at all times, as someone today might keep a ballpoint in a shirt pocket. When Caesar was attacked in the Roman senate on the Ides of March in 44 BC, he defended himself (according to Suetonius) with his stylus—in vain, of course: the sword in this case was mightier than the pen.

Soon after Caesar's time, for books and official documents, the graceful Roman Rustic script came into use—a domestic variant of Roman Square Capital. Its narrower strokes and contracted forms took up less space and so was less time-consuming and expensive to produce.

TESTATVRMORITVRADEOS·ET
SIDERA·TVMSIQVODNONAEQV
CVRAENVMENHABET·IVSTVM
NOXERAT·ETPIACIDVMCARPEB

Roman Rustic

The Romans used stylus-and-wax for brief or ephemeral bits of writing, like bills, personal correspondence, jottings, schoolwork,[2] but sometimes, surprisingly, they also used it to draw up legal documents like wills and contracts. The stuff was durable as long as you didn't leave it in the sun.

But for literary purposes, or anything they wished preserved *ad infinitum*, the ancients wrote with a brush made of hair, bristle, and various fibers, or with a calamus—a reed implement (*calamus* is the Latin word for *reed*) that was sharpened with a knife and split at the writing-end to facilitate the drawing up of the ink. This became the archetype of

2 Roman teachers would also spread sand on a table to teach letters and do sums, writing on it with a stick.

many subsequent pens, including the fountain pen with its split nib.

Modern calamus, hand-cut from a reed

Until around the fourth century, most writing was done on papyrus, which was made quite cheaply from reeds imported from Egypt. As a result, books were fairly inexpensive in Ancient Rome: you could pick up a copy of Martial's *Epigrams* for six sesterces. (As a comparison, Cleopatra's pearls were worth 40 million sesterces.)

Then, as the Roman Empire started to decline and, with it, trade between Rome and its colonies, including Egypt, parchment began to take the place of papyrus. It was made from a readily available source—animal skins, usually sheep—and had clear advantages over papyrus: parchment was much smoother and sturdier, and could be folded into the shape of something more like a book. The unwieldy scrolls we see in toga movies would have been papyrus.

The Uncial scripts[3] that grew out of Roman Square Capital were rounder, simpler, and more efficient—friendlier than the imposing Roman caps. Uncials were developed in the monasteries in answer to what the monks saw as an urgent need: just as Christianity was edging out paganism, the holier Uncial script began to replace its earlier Roman competitors, which, because they had been used for copying the works of pagan writers (Virgil, Horace, Cicero, Caesar himself), were considered sullied, and unsuitable for Church writings. (Even now, to me, Uncial has a hard-to-define but unmistakable "religious" look.)

One of Uncial's features was the introduction of small letters—not lower-case letters as we know them, but capitals written half their usual size, which saved paper and definitely

3 The origin of the word *uncial* in this context is obscure: the usage originated with St. Jerome in the preface to his translation of the Book of Job (c. 388) in which he refers to "unciales litteræ." The term is assumed to refer to the size of the letters (*uncia* means both "inch" and "ounce" in Latin), perhaps facetiously (i.e., they were big and bold), though it could also be either a misspelling or a misreading of Jerome's script.

sped things up. The variant known as Half-Uncial flirted with
true minuscule letters: the top loop of the *B* was eliminated, for
example, leaving the single-looped lower-case *b* we use today.

Nequediuentrumauctdifferent
quodcorporaltzerhabtzetinx
quidinhabtzatcorporaltzer

Roman Half-Uncial

The script was brought to Ireland by Bishop Patricius—aka St.
Patrick. The future bishop and saint was a Roman Briton, kid-
napped as a teenager and transported to Ireland to be a slave,
toiling for six years as a shepherd in what is now County Mayo.
He finally escaped, made his way home, was educated in monasteries, became a missionary, was consecrated a bishop, and
in the year 432 returned to Ireland—which during his captivity
he had come to love—to convert the pagan warrior chieftains
to Christianity. He also converted the Irish to Half-Uncial.

Over time, the Irish monks made their own improvements
and innovations as, doggedly copying manuscripts (the word
comes from the Latin *manu scriptis*, or *written by hand*) in their
scriptoria, they kept the flame of learning alive through the
so-called Dark Ages—a time of upheaval in Europe during
which, miraculously, handwriting flourished and spread. (The
period is now referred to more benignly by historians as Late
Antiquity or the Early Middle Ages.)

Gradually, the scripts that began to dominate were the
Irish spin-offs from Uncial, the so-called Insular Majuscule
and Insular Minuscule—*insular* because they were developed
on an island, *majuscule* because they consisted of all capital
letters. (Insular Minuscule, which included lower-case letters,
originated a little later, also in Ireland.) These highly pleasing

*The monastery
scriptorium*

scripts were taught by the Irish to the monks in Anglo-Saxon (i.e., English) monasteries, where the new forms caught on quickly. However, the old-fashioned Celtic churchmen, many of whom clung to the old Uncial scripts, were often at odds with the Anglo-Saxons, who were more enthusiastic embracers of what had become the official Christian establishment, based in Rome. The scripts the two factions favored coexisted peacefully enough, overlapping and influencing each other, but there were other problems: the Irish and Roman churches had differing calendars (so the date of Easter was always in dispute), they disagreed about whether penance should be performed in private or in public, and their monks favored opposing tonsure styles: the Anglo-Saxons shaved the tops of their heads, leaving the familiar neatly clipped monkish fringe, and ridiculed the Irish, who shaved the front half ear to ear and sported a long mane that hung down the back—a hairstyle possibly modeled on that of the Druids.

Essentially, it was a power struggle between progressives and conservatives. The backward-looking Celts lost: at the Synod of Whitby in 664, the issue was decided in favor of the Roman tradition, which dominates the Catholic Church to this day, and along with their wild hairstyles, the Irish monks' distinctive Uncial script was gradually replaced by its more compact Insular versions.

Te camt adcelebratque polis
rex zazirer hymnis trans
zephyrique globum scandunt
tuafacta per axem

Insular Minuscule, c. 700

It was during the course of the evolution of these scripts that the calamus—the reed pen—began to be seen as an inadequate writing implement. It had been a step forward from the brush, but because, like papyrus, it too had to be made from an imported reed, the calamus eventually fell into disuse, and a new writing implement appeared, one that would change the course of handwriting history.

THE QUILL

The idea of using bird feathers to write with had been around for centuries—between about 250 BC and 68 AD, the Dead Sea Scrolls were written, at least in part, with quills. But it wasn't until sometime in the late seventh or early eighth century that they became the major writing instrument in much of the world. The quill was versatile, flexible, and easier to manipulate than a brush. Its harder point—with a texture somewhat like the human fingernail—was better than the coarse tip of a calamus for writing on smooth parchment—but similar enough (hollow barrel, split nib) to be constructed easily by scribes. With the advent of the quill, handwriting became more varied and individual.

Quills were used for the illuminated manuscripts produced by monks in Ireland, including the *Lindisfarne Gospels* and the sumptuous *Book of Kells*. Anonymous wrote *Beowulf* with a quill and Chaucer *The Canterbury Tales*. Shakespeare wrote his thirty-seven plays and 154 sonnets with a quill. (At the New York Public Library shop, you can buy a Shakespeare action

The Well-Tempered Clavier

4 George Sand was prolific in everything she did: her correspondence has been collected into 25 volumes, she smoked like a chimney, and, according to her biographer, Belinda Jack, she even made jam in "ludicrous" quantities.

5 The pasta known as penne—Italian for "feathers"—actually look more like little writing instruments. The German word for pen is *Feder* and the French is *plume*, feathers all.

figure with a quill pen in one hand and a book in the other.) Martin Luther used a quill for his 95 Theses, Cervantes for *Don Quixote*, Bach for *The Well-Tempered Clavier*, Charles Perrault for "Cinderella," Mozart for *The Magic Flute*, Boswell for his *Life of Johnson*, Keats for the "Ode on a Grecian Urn," Jane Austen for *Pride and Prejudice*, Dickens for *Great Expectations*, Pushkin for *Eugene Onegin*. (A Russian three-ruble commemorative coin issued in 1999 bears on its reverse a portrait of Pushkin holding a quill.) George Sand wrote her staggering output of books, plays, and essays[4] in one room while Chopin composed his sublime nocturnes and mazurkas in another—both scratching away with their quill pens. The Magna Carta was written with a quill, and the Founding Fathers used one to put their John Hancocks on the Declaration of Independence. Presumably, your great-great-grandparents and mine signed their names (or perhaps just an X) with a quill pen.

Quills were within the reach of everyone—often right out in the barnyard. You could pluck a quill from the wing feathers (*penna* in Latin means *feather*)[5] of geese, turkeys, ravens (which could draw the finest lines), or (for the wealthy) swans. The best of them were plucked from living birds—pens for the right-handed from the left wing because of the way it curved, and vice versa.

The trouble with quill pens was that they lasted only about a week—for a compulsive scribbler, a mere day or two. There's a legend that the prolific Thomas Jefferson raised a special flock of geese at Monticello solely to satisfy his writing needs. I love this idea but, sadly, it does not seem to be true. The research librarian at the Jefferson library told me that geese were "one form of livestock that were typically purchased rather than raised" at the estate. On the other hand, there are no references in Jefferson's financial records to buying quill pens, either—so presumably he bought a goose when he needed one, plucked, and wrote.

You didn't have to make your quills from scratch—they were

Before

After: quills trimmed for writing

sold in quantity by street vendors and in stationery shops—
but many people did, even though they were a pain to prepare.
Once you managed to pluck a wing feather from a large, angry
bird (which—to anyone who's ever met up with a hissing swan—
sounds like the road to disaster), you had to cut away most of
the feathery bits to make the quill comfortable to hold.

Next, you had to harden it, a choice between burying it in
hot sand (a modern quillster recommends a soup-can of sand
in a 350 degree oven) or plunging it into a vat of acid (best to
do both). You fashioned the tip to the proper shape (an art in
itself), cut a slit in it, trimmed it into a nib, and scraped it
flat. Then, as you wrote with the thing, you had to fiddle with
it constantly to keep it sharp. (Hence, *penknife,* a tool also useful for erasing: a scribe could carefully scratch the ink off
the parchment with no harm done. Illustrations of medieval
scribes tend to show them with a quill in one hand and a knife
in the other.) No matter how careful you were, you could make
a cutting error and damage the quill badly with the knife, and,
once you did take pen in hand, drips and splatters of ink could
ruin your manuscript. And you might very well be doing all
this by candlelight.[6]

Presumably, people got the hang of it. The quill endured
for twelve centuries, and it made possible an awe-inspiring
array of scripts.

6 Harry Potter
sometimes performs
the awesome feat
of writing with a
quill and a bottle of
ink,on parchment,
under the covers with
a flashlight.

Carolingian Minuscule

The year 800, when Charlemagne was crowned Holy Roman Emperor, is widely seen as the dawn of the medieval era, a triumph for the spread of Christianity, and the start of a huge advance for education—and, trailing along with it, penmanship. Charlemagne (Carolus Magnus, 742–814) was the son of Pepin the Short, though he himself was taller than average. He was a strong, rugged, rough-and-ready warrior without much book learning—a princely good-time-Charlie who loved to eat.

Once he rose to power, he became a social reformer dedicated to improving the lives of his people, and interested, primarily, in education in all its aspects—including his own, which he had long neglected. With the scholar Alcuin of York (who had been summoned from England at the emperor's behest), Charlemagne encouraged government scribes and monks to adopt a new style of handwriting—a written lingua franca that could be recognized throughout his enormous empire. The new script was the first to slope gently to the right; it used lower case as well as capitals; and it included some connections between letters (which the quill could handle, but which would have been awkward for the less flexible calamus). For all these reasons it flowed more easily than its predecessors.

egrocacionem corporif accedat egr
Int ipfof quoq; fenfuf & omia mebra
caput. inquo uifuf &odorat.audit

Carolingian Minuscule

Unlike most of those, it also allowed for separations between words—something not considered attractive by writers of, for example, Roman Rustic—and it standardized punctuation, which had been inconsistent, haphazard, or completely nonexistent. Now the comma, quote marks, and question mark began to be used as we know them. The script came to be called Carolingian Minuscule, after the emperor—a nicely ironic historical note, since Charlemagne wrote a very poor hand despite all his efforts, though, unlike most rulers of his time, he was at least literate.

Gothic

The grace and readability of Carolingian Minuscule were severely compromised by the various Gothic scripts that succeeded it. What looks pointy, aggressive, and often impenetrable to our eyes must have been attractive and readable in the Middle Ages, because Gothic in its several incarnations was intensely popular. Whatever their faults, the Gothic scripts were neat and space-saving, and were the preferred bookhand—i.e., the script used for copying texts—in the thirteenth to fifteenth centuries, and even served as the basis of the first typefaces in printed books. Gothic came to be known as *blackletter* because a page of it was essentially a black sea of ink.

There were endless varieties of the script, some more pleasing than others—a lighter, less jagged and compressed version was known as *bastarda*, a generic term usually used for scripts that combined Gothic with a touch of cursive, and there are some beautiful offshoots in use today. But while many Gothics are lovely (albeit illegible), others—especially the later, exaggerated ones—share an unpleasantly crabbed, dense quality.[7] A monkish medieval joke is worth reproducing here, an exaggeration of Gothic's stodgy vertical illegibility:

Gothic script

7 They were termed "Gothic" by Renaissance scholars who found them as barbarous as the bloody and warlike Germanic tribe known as Goths—Gothic cathedrals were given the same sneering epithet. Plutarch said Gothic script was "pleasing to the eye but tiring to read."

8 This is from Marc Drogin's informative, entertaining, and useful book *Medieval Calligraphy: Its History and Technique*, which I recommend to anyone with even a passing interest in the subject.

It reads "Mimi numinum nivium minimi munium nimium vini muniminum imminui vivi minimum volunt," or "The very short mimes of the gods of snow do not at all wish that during their lifetime the very great burden of [distributing] the wine of the walls be lightened."[8]

Gothic scripts, perversely, emphasized the look of the entire word over the individual letter—the whole wrought-iron fence rather than the narrow gate that's an *n* or a *v*. Gothic was more about appearance than about legibility. And, in fact, the overall effect of a word or a sentence was quite grand—even if you held the page upside-down. (Try it with the example on the previous page.) In some variants, the letters were so closely woven they were called *textura*—textured. There are many textura styles, including *quadrata*—a favorite for newspaper titles, including the *New York Times*—whose letters have very precise diamond-shaped "feet"; *rotunda*, whose letters are more delicate, and rounded at the bottom; and *semi-quadrata*, with some rounded and some pointy feet.

Gothic looks like it was hell to write, but it persisted in Germany, where it was known as Fraktur, from the Latin *fractus* (for "fractured"): in some variations, the letter forms were not joined but broken up. In 1941 Hitler outlawed the script (calling it, with admirable illogic, "Jewish"), because people in Nazi-occupied territories couldn't read the propaganda disseminated by the Fraktur-writing Germans. However, it was never really eradicated, and the brutal, aggressive blackletter script is still associated with the Nazis.

But in general, as Gothic became ever more elaborate, and burdened with endless regional reworkings, people turned once more to less intricate, more legible styles.

This syndrome characterizes much of the history of handwriting, which has been driven at least partly by the tension between aesthetics and utility. Writing designed primarily for business—writing that, in effect, had a built-in deadline—has traditionally been about speed and legibility. Writing used for literary or religious purposes could be more leisurely and hence more decorative, driven by the simple desire for beauty—or showmanship. "If it ain't broke, don't fix it" has no relevance here: a plain and practical script was no sooner introduced than it would be dolled up by scribes, who worked variations on a theme. After a while the original began to seem uninteresting or just plain ugly, and the fittest variation that survived became standard. In turn, that would become too ordinary, and users with an artistic eye made further changes until a new script was born. Some were a reaction against too much flash, some against too much austerity. There were revivals in handwriting history—romantic throwbacks to a supposedly better age—just as there were in the history of art and architecture. But the process meant that handwriting over the centuries went through a vast number of transformations.

Italic Writing

The Italic (a term that honors its Italian origins) or "secretary hand" (i.e., used by clerks) emerged toward the end of the fifteenth century:

It became popular not only with clerks but with educated writers of the time because it was more in tune with the humanist ideals of the Renaissance, part of the turning away from the barbaric extremes of Gothic sensibility. The slanty *italic* we use for emphasis on a printed page comes from Italic script.

Italic first appeared in Venice c. 1500, the inspiration of either a printer named Aldus Manutius or his type-cutter, Francesco Griffo (or possibly a collaboration by both). It was, in Manutius's words, "an entirely new design." The pocket edition of Virgil in which Manutius introduced it was a sensational bestseller, and Italic quickly spread all over Europe. It was probably the hand used by Shakespeare.[9]

As the handwriting historian A. S. Osley speculated in his article "Origins of Italic Type," Italic's popularity may have been aided by the fact that, in the early days of printed books, the stiff and upright Roman type that, by then, was usually the choice of printers "was monotonous to eyes attuned to the irregularities of manuscript." Italic, which used some ligatures (i.e., connected letters) and had a natural rightward slant even in its printed form, was meant to imitate the rapid, improvised cursive scrawl of the average hand-writer.

Italic was, of course, far more pleasing and elegant than any vernacular writing style. As it evolved, it combined some of the better features of the Italian version of Gothic script—European nostalgia for Gothic was inexplicable but undeniable—with a touch of the graceful and clearly defined Carolingian letterforms that represented the characteristically Renaissance nostalgia for the glories of the ancient world.

Between 1440 and 1500, about 40,000 books were produced on European presses. As the printing press began to take over the making of books—or of anything that needed to exist in multiple copies—the need for professional scribes diminished. A case in point is Antonio Sinibaldi (1443–1528), one of the most famous scribes of the early Italian Renaissance. His masterpiece—and the high point of his career—was a commission to letter the text of a particularly magnificent Book of Hours for Lorenzo de Medici.[10] But by 1480 Sinibaldi was complaining in a note on his tax return that he was so broke he could hardly afford to keep himself clothed.

In reaction to the job crisis, many practical-minded scribes became writing masters, teaching fine penmanship skills to the educated classes—a new profession that provided the best of them with an excellent living. The writing masters also found a way to capitalize on the printing press: they began producing their own printed how-to books, prepared using wood blocks cut from their original designs.

The books—delightful objects in themselves—sold well, and elegant handwriting quickly became the rage, especially among the burgeoning clerical class. As Osley puts it in his book *Scribes and Sources*, "During the sixteenth century bureaucracy really began to flourish in Europe. The new offices had to be manned [and] young men of good family could find satisfying careers in this line of business." All these eager young strivers—the yuppies of their day—needed to be taught a legible and pleasing hand.

As both teachers and designers of scripts, the Italian masters were highly influential. The greatest were Giambattista Palatino, who is considered by many to be the greatest calligrapher who ever lived, and Ludovico Vicentino Arrighi, who created the first printed handwriting manual in 1522, the startlingly beautiful *La Operina*:

Farai che' la distantia da linea a linea de cose' che' scriuiera in tal littera Cancellaresca non sui troppo larga, ne' troppo stretta

Before Arrighi's death in 1527 (he perished in the sack of Rome by the Holy Roman Emperor Charles V), he wrote, designed, and printed a detailed treatise on quills, with tips on selecting and cutting them, choosing inkwells (the best ones were of lead because it keeps the ink fresh), ink (it's best to mix your own, in small batches), and a penknife (make sure it's of well-tempered steel, with a sturdy, comfortable handle), not to mention various tools—thimbles, lamps, rulers, tweezers, shears, etc.—that were indispensable for the serious penman.

More than three centuries later, Arrighi's work would serve as a model for William Morris during the nineteenth-century Arts and Crafts calligraphy revival.[11] Oscar Wilde reported that, at an exhibition in London, "a photographic projection of a page of Arrighi was greeted with a spontaneous round of applause."

Italic in the more formal version known as *cancellaresca* (chancery hand) was used in the courts of the Vatican. (Arrighi worked in the Apostolic Chancery copying papal briefs until he was fired for his attempts to battle the graft and corruption that flourished there.) Chancery hand lacked Italic's characteristic rightward slope, and—like other scripts meant for legal use—was sometimes deliberately illegible to keep the wrong people from reading (or forging) confidential texts:

Chancery hand

However, though they retained some of chancery's stateliness, the more readable, right-slanting Italic forms prevailed, and the script became renowned for its clarity, answering a demand for a refined, useful, and historically valid script not only for bureaucrats but among the educated classes in general.

11 The Arts and Crafts movement was a reaction against the perceived "soullessness" of manufactured goods, including commercial publishing. The leader of the movement, William Morris—himself a calligrapher, printer, and textile designer as well as a poet and artist—was a fervent champion of calligraphy and other traditional arts.

With the rise of Italic, there was a slowing of the persistent changes that had characterized script styles for a thousand years. One of Italic's virtues was its relative speediness, but because technology in the form of the printing press had taken over mass production of manuscripts, scribes no longer had to tailor the prevailing script to massive writing projects. Fast copying became less important. As a result, professional penmen were now teachers and craftsmen more than they were innovators: their task was to refine, sustain, and disseminate their skills.

Copperplate

It goes without saying that, useful and popular though it was, Italic script did not answer the needs of every writer, but the post-Renaissance changes were about neither art nor speed: they were about morality. For Puritans and other reformers in England and America, the scripts favored in Europe were too elaborate, too baroque—perhaps too seductively gorgeous—and the plain and easy script known as *copperplate* (or *roundhand*) was devised as an alternative. By the eighteenth century, roundhand—so called because it was structured on the shape of the letter *O*—was in wide use.[12]

12 The word *copperplate* is often misunderstood as a generic term for fancy, old-fashioned handwriting. In Thomas Harris's *Hannibal*, Hannibal Lecter is said to have copperplate handwriting. A character named Dr. Doemling comments: "You see that sort of handwriting in medieval papal bulls." But copperplate, of course, was a far later phenomenon, unknown to medieval prelates.

English roundhand, 1736

Roundhand was versatile: it was used for printing as well as handwriting, and though its standard forms were designed for business, it allowed for a daintier style suitable for ladies. Furthermore, if the writer was so inclined, and unconstrained by religious strictures—in other words, if the writer was a professional penman whose chief obsession was with his craft—roundhand could be endlessly embellished with fancy swirls and shadings. The process was accelerated by an instrument that was just being introduced: the flexible pointed pen, whose dainty point provided an alternative to the traditional blunt nib, which was shaped like a small screwdriver. At first, these finer pens were used only as drawing implements, and when the penmen took them up it was small wonder that their scripts began to undergo "the transformation of ordinary handwriting into a performing art," as Charles L. Lehman put it in *Handwriting Models for Schools* (1976).

Most ordinary writers continued to use the ubiquitous quill, and were still writing the Gothic-tinged Italic that was the norm. But penmen in England, and eventually the colonies (particularly Boston and Philadelphia), were more interested in roundhand and the extremes to which it could be taken. I have a facsimile copy of George Bickham's *The Universal Penman*, a 1743 collection of sample scripts by twenty-five notable English penmen of the day, including Bickham himself. In his introduction, Bickham warns against excessive flourishing, and is critical of too many "turns of the pen" that "seem rather designed to fill up Vacancies on the Paper than studiously compos'd to adorn the Piece."

The tolerance for such embellishment must have been fairly high in the 1740s. Bickham includes a relatively straightforward selection of alphabets—not only roundhand but Roman, Italic, Court Hand, Old English (which looks suspiciously like Gothic), and even "Arabick" and "Syriack":

ARABICK.

اَلسَّلَامُ لَكِ يَامَرْيَمُ الْمُمْتَلِيَةَ مِنَ اللُّغَةِ الرَّبُّ
مَعَكِ مُبَارَكَةٌ اَنْتَ فِي النِّسَاءُ وَمُبَارَكَةٌ
ثَمَرُ بَطْنِكِ يَسُوعَ *

SYRIACK.

ܠܦܘܕܘܝܣ ܚܝܨܪܐ ܘܨܐܘܢܣܐ ܘܚܘܠܐ ܠܐ
ܐܢܚܪ : ܟܨܚܢܣܐ ܘܣܟܡܣܐ ܠܐ ܗܪ. ܗܠܐ
ܗܘܐܚܐ ܘܗܟܬܢܩܫܐ ܠܐ ܟܐܚ ܀

But this was, after all, the age of rococo, and everything from hairstyles to silversmithing was way over the top. The glory of Bickham's book is its flourishes, which abound—as do scrolls, spirals, frames, flowers, doves, and *putti*:

Lucius seems fond of Life; but what is Life?
'Tis not to stalk about, and draw fresh Air
From time to time, or gaze upon the Sun;
'Tis to be Free. When Liberty is gone,
Life grows insipid, and has lost its Relish.

Despite their excesses, the accomplishments of the eighteenth-century quillmeisters look mighty impressive to the modern eye. My own experience of paging through Bickham and taking notes in my ungainly modern scribble was instructive. Marc Drogin reminded me that most of these elaborate early scripts were not "handwriting" as we know it: "They were 'display lettering,' slowly produced elaborate declarative lettering that announced its own importance. It is the quick sloppy cursives that were used at the same time—for lists and notes, personal notebooks or florilegia,[13] the second and third copies of court records—that were 'handwriting.'"

13 Literary anthologies containing the "flowers," or absolute best, culled from one's personal reading.

Still, as Jackson points out in *The Story of Writing*, "Kings, clerks, and educated men and women everywhere imitated the style of the writing masters." What a different world it was, when a supremely legible but elegant script was the standard to which everyone, in some measure at least, aspired. If we try to imagine what it was like to receive in the mail a bill that looked like this:

Sᵣ Pargiter Fleetwood, Dᵣ.

To James Mainstone for Work & Materials in his House on Tower-Hill, London.

1738.

Mar. 28. Bricks	25 thousᵈ.	at 15:7 ℔ M.	£ 19 . 9 . 7
30 . Tiles	11 Ditto.	at 19 : 5 Ditto.	10 . 13 . 7
Apr. 5 . Lime	28 hund.	at 15 : 11 ℔ hund	22 . 5 . 8
12 . Sand	19 Load.	at 3 : 10 ℔ Load	3 . 12 . 10
May, 7 . Ridge Tiles	149	at 8 : 1 ℔ hund	_ . 12 , _
June, 16 . Work, for self.	90 Days,	at 3 : _ ℔ diem	13 . 10 . _
_ . Dᵒ. y Labourer.	90 Dᵒ.	at 1 : 8 Ditto.	7 . 10 . _
_ . Dᵒ. my Man.	90 Dᵒ.	at 2 : 6 Ditto.	11 . 5 . _

£ . 88 . 18 . 8

N.B. A Brick ought to be 9 Inches long, 4¼ broad, & 2½ thick. 500 Bricks are a Load, a thousand Tiles the same. 25 Bushels are a hundred of Lime. About 4500 Bricks will make a Rod of Brickwork, Viz. 272¼ Square Feet, a Brick & a half thick.

instead of like this:

Charge details		
Previous balance		$170.74
12/12 Payment - Thank You		-150.74
Comcast Cable Television		$111.85
12/28 - 1/27 Cable/internet/phone Pkg		99.00
Special 12 Month Promotion Includes: Comcast Digital Starter Package - A Variety Of Programming For Everyone In The Home; Comcast High - Speed Internet - Blazing Download Speeds; Comcast Digital Voice - Unlimited Direct-dial Domestic Local/Id Calling.		
12/28 - 1/27 Franchise Related Cost		0.86
(Cost Associated With Local Access Programming, Facilities, Equipment Or Other Related License Requirements)		
12/28 - 1/27 Digital Classic		6.20
Includes: Digital Classic, Digital Music Choice, Interactive Program Guide.		
Cable Television monthly charges		$105.86
11/28 8:14p Factotum		5.99
On-Demand and Pay-Per-View		$5.99
Comcast Digital Voice		$7.95
12/28 - 1/27 Voice/data Equipment		3.00
Digital Voice monthly charges		$3.00
Domestic Calls		0.00
Operator Svcs/dir Asst.		3.96
Per-call charges		$3.96
Univ. Connectivity Chg.- Usage		0.09
Univ. Connectivity Chg.- Recurring		0.51
Tot. Univ. Connectivity Chg.		$0.60
Regulatory Recovery Fees - Usage		0.00

Comcast Digital Voice (cont.)	
The Regulatory Recovery Fee is not a government mandated charge. It defrays regulatory costs such as state universal services, relay services, 911, and state/local utility fees.	
View Voice & Mobile Access Detail at www.comcast.com/viewbill	
One-time charges and credits	-$20.00
12/17 $20 Cert 205706 Applied - Adjustment	-20.00
Taxes, surcharges and fees	$7.79
Cable Television	
State Of Connecticut Tax	2.90
FCC Fee	0.06
Gross Receipts Tax	2.40
Digital Voice	
State Sales	2.19
Per-call Taxes	0.24
Total due by 01/15/07	$127.59

Important Account Information

If you have already contacted Comcast at 1-888-824-2273 and you remain dissatisfied with Comcast's resolution to your complaint, you may contact the CT DEPARTMENT OF PUBLIC UTILITY CONTROL, Consumer Assistance Unit, Ten Franklin Square, New Britain, CT 06051. The Department

we can begin to comprehend what changes 350-odd years of culture have wrought, and to understand—despite the belief that the makeup of humans stays essentially the same over the centuries—what a vast gulf there is between the world we live in and the London world of 1743.

Fashions in script—like the latest bonnet styles—traveled swiftly across the ocean; the work of the English writing masters was enormously influential in the colonies. Roundhand is usually known in America as copperplate, from the fact that, in addition to being written by hand, this was the script that was etched into copper plates for printing by an engraver. It's the handwriting familiar to us on all the crucial American documents: the Declaration of Independence, once past its fancy Gothic heading, is all copperplate.

Benjamin Franklin, a penmanship buff,[14] wrote an elegant hand that wouldn't have made it into Bickham, but was certainly of a high standard—and check out that signature:

14 The typeface used by, among others, the Museum of Modern Art, is named after him: Franklin Gothic—though it seems about as Ben-like as the MoMA building resembles Independence Hall.

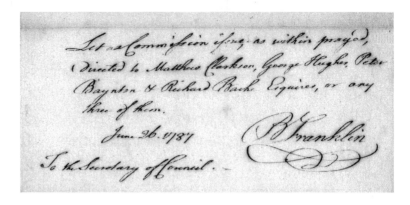

Franklin included instructions for producing a nifty copperplate in his 1748 book, *The American Instructor*, which also contained helpful advice on "how to write letters on business or friendship"—such things were so codified at the time, they were almost ritualistic. Samuel Richardson's *Pamela, or, Virtue Rewarded* (1740) might never have come into existence had Richardson, at that time a printer, not been asked by a London bookseller to come up with a book on letterwriting. The unexpected result was a novel in letters—the racy, best-selling tale of a teenage serving maid who, in her reports home to her parents, describes her successful attempt to escape seduction (read: rape) by her employer, save her virtue, and—in the end—get the cad to marry her. (The story is implausible, sexist, preachy, often hilarious, and, in the end, deeply satisfying.)

In his own much more serious handbook, Franklin is reassuring on the subject of the limitations of the average human—he writes that "those who aim at perfect Writing by imitating the engraved copies, tho' they never reach the wish'd for Excellence…, their Hand [i.e., their handwriting] is mended by the Endeavor, and is tolerable while it continues fair & legible." He was convinced of the value of a good script, and, when he founded the Academy of Philadelphia (which later became the University of Pennsylvania), Franklin stipulated that, if a young man wished to be admitted, he must "write a legible hand."

Admission must have been pretty exclusive. In colonial America it was considered necessary for just about everyone, including a substantial percentage of slaves, to be literate enough to read the Bible. (Religious slaveowners were some-times torn between their desire to spread the word of God and their belief that Africans were not actually human.) White children were taught to read at home by their mothers as they were taught to tie their shoes; both were important life skills.

But handwriting was something else. Only rich folks and businessmen learned to write, or even to read handwriting. For the average person, script was like an alien alphabet, as foreign to a colonial housewife (who could probably decipher printed texts with ease) as Chinese would be today—and as unnecessary. (And, even if they'd been grudgingly taught to read, slaves were discouraged from learning to write, lest they communicate escape plans to each other or try to contact the outside world.) As public schooling became more common, writin' began to be taught along with readin' (and 'rithmetic), but, although the Puritans in New England were supporting schools as early as the 1640s, this was a slow process. It wasn't until after the turn of the nineteenth century that schooling (at least to the eighth grade) became universal, with hand-writing taught as part of the curriculum.

As it passed through all its historic stages, writing as practiced by the average person gradually evolved into some-thing more than a purely utilitarian tool—pleasing penman-ship became a sign of gentility. For a while, some wealthy men affected illegible handwriting to show that they were too important and leisured to bother with such piddling concerns. Most of the wastrels—and there are many—in eighteenth- and nineteenth-century novels write an arrogant scrawl. The tradition goes back at least as far as Hamlet, who saw good handwriting as a sign of base birth.

But eventually, as the nouveau riche supplanted old money, an excellent and readable script, the mark of a shrewd businessman, became the indicator of worth—much as an artfully designed and easily navigable computer setup might be today.

METAL PENS

When quills began, finally, to be superseded by metal pens and pen-points in the nineteenth century, there must have been some rejoicing, and not only in the bird world. I imagine that many writers must have felt the way they did when the "word processor" came along: life suddenly got easier. In his humorous poem "Ode to Perry" (a pen manufacturer), Thomas Hood wrote in 1825 about "times begone, when each man cut his quill":

> What horrid, awkward, bungling tools of trade
> Appeared the writing instrument, home-made!

The metal nib was patented in 1803. The summer before that, the poet Coleridge took off on a nine-day walking/writing tour among the peaks of the Lake District, carrying six quills and a portable inkwell. Four years later, his friend Wordsworth wrote an eighteen-page letter to a friend—a feat he claimed was pos-sible because he'd received a steel pen as a gift. By that date Jefferson, who loved gadgets, was beginning to phase out the quill pen and had become deeply attached to what was called a "polygraph machine," which automatically made copies of what he wrote using a second metal pen attached to the pen he was using, like a phantom second arm. The copies it made were amazingly accurate: Jefferson called it "the finest inven-tion of the present age." Metal pen variations soon included the oblique penholder, which facilitates the arcs and shading of ornamental penmanship.

Oblique penholder

But metal pens, which had to be imported from England, were difficult to manufacture, and expensive. They were made laboriously by hand until the screw-press was perfected, which enabled them to be stamped out by machine, rounded—and split. That was the tricky part: the nib had to approximate the flexibility of the quill, yet be durable and also hold the ink properly. In addition, new inks had to be developed—the acid-based inks then in existence corroded the metal points.

Gradually, manufacturers worked out the glitches. But metal pens were slow to be accepted by the American public. No doubt there were writers who clung to their quills. Dickens was one: according to an early biographer, he "invariably wrote with a quill pen and blue ink"—blue because it dried faster. One can imagine people complaining that the new invention was cold, unnatural, newfangled, and gimmicky, with a tendency to tear the paper if you weren't careful—just as, a bit later, some writers resisted first the typewriter and then the computer. But in fact metal pens were infinitely sturdier and easier to use, and could perform more tricks on the page—this was the heyday of copperplate and then Spencerian[15] script. They also required virtually no upkeep: pen knives could now be used for carving your initials into desk tops. The new pens gradually became indispensable.

Metal pens arrived in America in 1856 when Richard Esterbrook set up a factory in New Jersey. By the end of that century, only fuddy-duddy Luddites were still using quills.[16]

15 The handwriting of nineteenth-century America. (See Chapter Two.)

16 As I write these words, I wonder if *fuddy-duddy*, whose origin, says the dictionary, is "unknown," is in fact an offshoot of *Luddite*—the kind of facetious mangling that turns *little* into *itty-bitty*.

FOUNTAIN PENS

As the twentieth century turned, script remained fairly static. The written forms of the letters of the alphabet were essentially those we're familiar with today. But pen history suddenly speeded up. After long, leisurely centuries of inkwells and dip pens in various forms, a truly innovative writing implement was introduced: the fountain pen.

The so-called "reservoir pen" had probably been around, in a half-hearted way, for a thousand years or so, lingering tantalizingly on the fringes of pen history but never quite surfacing as a viable writing method. But in the full flower of the industrial age, such pen giants as Waterman, Parker, Sheaffer, and Cross figured out how to make a pen that was easy to fill and that worked on the principle of what Donald Jackson in *The Story of Writing* calls "the controllable leak." (The crucial word was *controllable*: early fountain pens tended to leak not neatly

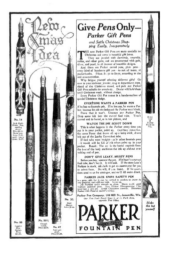

*Mont Blanc
"Le Grand"*

17 With the "51," Parker
   began numbering its
   pens as a response
   to the growing export
   market. Numbers didn't
   need translation.

onto the page when called upon, but messily into the pocket at odd moments.) The path to perfection was littered with disasters. An eyedropper was used at first to dribble the ink into the reservoir, with predictable results. It was followed by the click filler (it clicked when the pen was full), the matchstick filler (stick a matchstick through a hole to depress a rubber ink sac), and the coin filler (depress the sac with a coin).

The first successful fountain pen appeared in 1897, Conklin's rather bulky Crescent-Filler, which required the user to depress, then release, a raised half-moon to begin the ink flow. That was followed in 1906 by a Waterman version that concealed the filling mechanism with a sliding sleeve. But with the development in 1908 of Sheaffer's enduring lever-filler—the pen of my youth, with its internal rubber ink sac depressed by a metal lever—the fountain pen era had truly arrived.

Pen manufacturers, like the scribes before them, didn't stop tinkering with the design. The innovative piston-filler came along in the 1920s, activated with wonderful ease by the turning of a knob at the end of the pen to push down the piston, then pull it up again to draw in the ink. The Mont Blanc "Le Grand," unchanged for sixty years and still one of the company's most expensive pens, is a piston-filler.

A variation was the Parker Vacumatic, introduced in 1933, which sucked a large supply of ink swiftly into the pen's barrel by creating a vacuum with several strokes of a tiny spring-loaded pump at the back end. The Parker "51,"[17] the most popular fountain pen ever made, used a Vacumatic filler, but by 1948 it was passé: the new, highly alkaline inks, fast-drying but caustic, tended to corrode the Vacumatic's rubber diaphragm. The company replaced it with a very simple system that filled the pen when the user pushed and released a spring bar that depressed a clear plastic sac—an updated version of Waterman's forty-year-old sleeve filler.

Then there was the Snorkel, launched by Sheaffer in 1952. The Snorkel pen, which used a pneumatic mechanism called the Touchdown to draw in the ink like a tiny soda straw, got a huge boost in the 1950s when the actress Vivian Vance, famous as Ethel Mertz on the *I Love Lucy* show, appeared in a commercial. Yakking on the phone with Lucy, Ethel says she bought her husband, Fred, one of the pens for Christmas—he has a ballpoint but he needs a fountain pen for "important stuff." We cut from Ethel's blonde ditziness to a shot of her hands twisting the pen: "A special filling tube comes out and it drinks up the ink. Not even Fred could get his hands messy with this pen!"

Sheaffer Snorkel

A Fred-and-Ethel-vintage mint-condition "White Dot" Snorkel pen can now be found for between $100 and $150—a small price to pay for a sublime slice of nostalgia—and, as I recall, a very good pen.

Today, fountain pens are a marginal market, but they haven't entirely disappeared. The Levenger ("Tools for Serious Readers") catalog has a good line of not-too-expensive ones—along with cunning little doodads for carrying them, storing them, filling them, and displaying them. Even my neighborhood Staples sells not only the disposable Pilot Varsity fountain pen, but a deluxe Cross pen (not as pretty as you'd think), a Waterman Philéas (nicer), and a truly splendid black lacquer Waterman Expert II that I would love to own.

New fountain pens now run the price gamut from $2.20 for the Pilot disposable to $9,349 for the Waterman Sérénité line: solid silver body and 18k gold nib, with trim in your choice of

Laszlo Biro

crocodile skin, quail shell, mother of pearl, or gold dust. I'd like to pit the Varsity against the Sérénité in a write-off to see how much difference $9,346.80 makes in my handwriting, but that is probably not going to happen in this life.

BALLPOINTS

In 1938, a Hungarian journalist named Laszlo Biro invented the ballpoint pen.

Biro was a journalist who noticed that the ink being used to print newspapers dried instantly and didn't smudge, and he set out to devise a pen that would perform equally well. He soon discovered that he'd have to invent a new kind of pen point to handle the thick, sludgy ink. With the help of his brother George, a chemist, he fitted a tiny rolling metal ball to the tip, and the ballpoint was born. In 1940, the Biro brothers fled the Nazis and relocated to Argentina, where they patented the pen in 1943 and began manufacturing it. Biro is so highly respected in Argentina that their Inventor's Day is celebrated on his birthday, September 29.

His invention was adopted by the Royal Air Force in England,[18] which commissioned the pens for use during World War II because they didn't leak (or explode) at high altitudes, as fountain pens did.

18 Where a ballpoint is still called a biro, pronounced "bye-ro."

However, the ballpoint pen was not perfect. Despite its contribution to the war effort, it failed to capture the public imagination because early versions did, in fact, leak, whatever your altitude. The nuns at my school scorned ballpoints as sloppy, unnecessary, and probably sinful. They also tended to skip. And they were dreadfully expensive: a decent fountain pen could be had for a dollar, a ballpoint cost $3.95 and up.

But pen makers persevered and, as we all know, the ballpoint won the pen wars. In 1950, Michel Bich, a French baron, came up with the idea for a completely disposable pen that was cheap to produce. Today, Bic sells fifty-seven of them with

every tick of the clock. Rollerball pens use the same principle as the ballpoint: a ball bearing, ceramic rather than metal,
dispenses ink as it rolls across the page—but the ink involved
is a water-based liquid, like the ink in a fountain pen, rather
than the oily, viscous ink of a ballpoint. Gel pens, another
ballpoint-esque implement, use the same mechanism but the
ink is much thicker and more vibrant.

There's a popular myth that NASA spent "millions" of dollars developing a pen for astronauts to use in the weightless
environment of a space ship—while their sensible Russian
counterparts were happly to use the low-tech pencil. Alas, for
all its appeal and plausibility, this is not true. Initially, astronauts and cosmonauts were both equipped with pencils, but
there were problems: if a piece of lead broke off, for example,
it could float into someone's eye or nose. A pen was needed,
one that would defy gravity, write in extreme heat or cold, and
be leakproof: blobs of ink floating around the cabin would be
more perilous than a stray pencil lead. A long-time pen maker
named Paul C. Fisher patented the "space pen" in 1965 (which
he had developed at the cost of a million dollars, at the request
of but not under the auspices of NASA). NASA bought four
hundred of them at $6 each and, after a couple of years of test-
ing, the pens were put into space.

They worked just fine, occasionally in unexpected roles.
On the Apollo 11 flight in 1969, as the astronauts were about to
blast off in their lunar lander to head home from the moon,
they inadvertently damaged the starter switch. Their tool kit
was part of the gear they'd left behind on the lunar surface;
the crew was already sealed in and couldn't get out to go back
for it. What to do? Somebody back at Mission Control thought
that maybe the casing of a space pen would do in a pinch. It did.
Mission accomplished.

The famous smeariness of ballpoint has acquired an
un-usual modern use: fund-raisers and telemarketers are

Fisher
"Space Pen"

beginning to phase out those phony-looking computer fonts that address envelopes in what is supposed to look like script. Everybody's on to them. Instead, they've begun hiring actual humans to write the addresses in ballpoint, whose crude authenticity can't be faked by a machine:

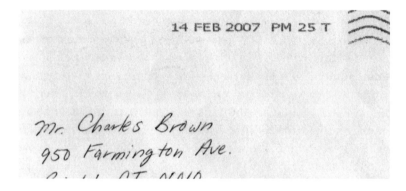

Expert penmanship is not called for, apparently—only legibility; the clumsier and more earnest the handwriting, the more convincing it is. As the head of a telemarketing firm puts it, "We realized the degree of personalization corresponded to fulfillment and response rates"—which presumably means that the scheme is working.

INK

The ink that has been used over the centuries to power all these writing implements would fill a small ocean. From its murky depths has emerged everything from the Bible to yesterday's spelling test.

Ink has been made from soot mixed with gelatin, soot mixed with vinegar, soot mixed with glue, the secretions of squid, the secretions of cuttlefish, crushed flowers, dried beetles, walnuts, iron salts, copper salts, tannin, oak galls, hawthorn bark mixed with wine, elderberries, pokeberries, blueberries, blackberries, raspberries, indigo, pomegranate seeds, blood, and (for that delight of nine-year-olds, invisible ink) lemon juice.

The Chinese, for whom good ink was one of the "four precious things of the study" (along with pen, paper, and inkstone), came up with a solid ink made of soot and gelatin (made from boiled animal skins) dried into a cake: a writer would grind a small piece on an inkstone and mix it with water to the preferred consistency. The Romans made a purple *encaustum* (from which we get the word *ink*) from iron salts and oak galls, and a pound of it cost the equivalent of five cents—about the same as a quart of sheep's milk or half a dozen artichokes. A Roman barber made a penny per haircut, a stonemason took home about twenty-two cents a month, and a scribe was paid not quite eleven cents for a hundred lines of his best writing. At that price, encaustum wasn't available to most Romans. But of course most Romans couldn't write, anyway.

For use with his printing press, the inventive Gutenberg devised a mixture of soot and linseed oil that was thick enough to adhere to the type and black enough not to fade; similar oil-based inks are still used today for printing presses and in print cartridges. The ink recipe devised by Isaac Newton (scientist, mathematician, natural philosopher, and alchemist, 1643–1727) involved soaking tannin and gum Arabic[19] in beer, fermenting it for a month, then adding ferrous sulfate, letting it stand in the sun, and voilà: a lovely black ink that tended to age to a warm brown. To combat the ink shortage during the Civil War, Confederate soldiers made their own by boiling rusty nails in vinegar. Modern do-it-yourselfers prefer either strong tea mixed with gum Arabic, or a mix of walnuts, salt, and vinegar, boiled and strained. When I mistakenly steamed a batch of cranberry shell beans in their pods instead of shelling them first, I was left with a pan of rosy-red juice, and I boiled it down to make a very credible ink.

By the time Waterman put ink into handy plastic cartridges in the mid-'50s—another substantial leap forward—ink in bottles became increasingly hard to find. (Not that it mattered: by then, fountain pens were on their way out.) At Sta-

19 An edible, water soluble substance derived from the sap of the acacia tree, still used today, not just in inks—to increase viscosity—but in aspirin, crayons, and marshmallows, and Gummi Bears. In Africa, it's used to feed livestock and cure the common cold.

ples, a clerk and I searched in vain for a bottle of ink ("Jeez, I thought we had some in aisle five...."). Ink is readily available in art supply stores—artists and calligraphers are the main customers. But for the average person, ink is now an artifact of another world.

PENCILS

Pencils haven't scratched out much of a role in the world of penmanship. It's hard to produce truly memorable script with a pencil. Maybe it's psychological: the humble work of the pencil seems ephemeral, easily destroyed by a mere eraser. And yet there's no question that much handwriting—the utilitarian, list-making kind—is done with a pencil. What, after all, would we do without them? For a true handwriting nut, they have their place in the pantheon of writing implements, even if it is way down at the end past the cheap, smeary ballpoint and just this side of the wax crayon.

The history of pencil making has been documented by Henry Petroski in *The Pencil: A History of Design and Circumstance*. It's a brain-crushingly exhaustive but surprisingly absorbing book, and I recommend it highly. But for our present purposes, I will attempt to present the pencil's impressive lineage in a quick sketch.

Pencils date back to the Middle Ages, when they were made of soft lead wrapped with twine or wool. Then, in the sixteenth century, in the town of Borrowdale, near Keswick in northern England, a tree blew down in a storm and unearthed a cache of what was thought at first to be lead but was actually graphite—a form of carbon[20]—by a group of shepherds. Legend has it that they used it to mark their sheep until someone (either an Italian or a German, depending on which history you read) got the hang of encasing graphite in strips of wood, and the modern pencil was born.

20 In Borrowdale, with appropriate Olde World picturesqueness, it was called simply "wad." Then it was known as "plumbago"—a form of carbon—but it came to be called "graphite" from *graphos*, the Greek word for writing.

For a long time pencils were a steady cottage industry in Keswick, first made entirely by hand by the villagers, then in small factories, and exported all over the world.

The Derwent Pencil Factory in Keswick

But over the centuries the Borrowdale mine's pure graphite—the only source known—began to be exhausted, and as the substance became rare, England lost its monopoly on pencil making. In 1795 France, Nicolas Jacques Conté, whose well-known Conté crayons are still prized by artists, added clay to graphite to create a new writing substance that was not only cheap but, according to how much graphite it contained, either hard or soft. Shortly after, in Germany, Lothar von Faber, manufacturer of the first brand-name pencil (and still a famous name in the pencil world), standardized the now-ubiquitous hexagonal pencil—i.e., a pencil that would not roll off the desk but still was comfortable to hold. And in 1847, a French adventurer named Jean Pierre Alibert, panning for gold in Siberia, happened upon unpromising black chunks of stuff that turned out to be graphite as pure as that from Borrowdale. The mine he eventually built on the Chinese-Siberian border became as profitable as gold, which is why pencils started being painted the golden yellow we're familiar with today.

Sometime around 1800, an enterprising American schoolgirl—whose name, unfortunately, has not survived—apparently began making pencils for herself and her friends by hollowing out an elder twig with a knitting needle and stuffing it with graphite from pencil stubs that she pounded to a pulp and mixed with glue. But it wasn't until the War of 1812, when trade with England ceased, that Americans entered in earnest upon the manufacture of pencils. The first American pencil was sold just before the fourth of July in that year. It was made in Concord, Massachusetts, which became a thriving pencil-making center when a lode of impure but serviceable graphite was found in New Hampshire in 1821 by Charles Dunbar, who was the brother of Henry David Thoreau's mother, Cynthia. Charles Dunbar and John Thoreau, Henry's father, started manufacturing pencils in a shed behind the Thoreau house.

The flawed American graphite was notoriously brittle and gritty but it made for a pencil that was cheaper than imported ones, and good enough for the average user. In 1837, fresh out of Harvard (where pencil profits had sent him), Henry David Thoreau—who had helped out in the family business from childhood—applied his intelligence and ingenuity to figuring out a way to mix graphite with clay instead of with wax, glue, and spermaceti, which was the current practice. (Conté's formula hadn't crossed the ocean.) He also devised a machine for grinding the graphite more finely to reduce grit.[21] By all accounts, the Thoreaus started to make some pretty nifty pencils—they won the Massachusetts Charitable Mechanic Association

21 Thoreau was nothing if not ingenious: in addition to his pencil innovations, he not only built his famous cabin at Walden Pond, but is said to have invented raisin bread.

Inside label of an original Thoreau pencil box

award for excellence in 1847 and 1849—and they sold well, even though they were costly: twenty-five cents each, as opposed to about a nickel for inferior pencils. In 2006, two Thoreau & Son pencils (one sharpened, one not) sold in a Massachusetts auction for $2,088 to a Maryland bookseller with a serious Thoreau collection.

A typical pencil can draw a line thirty-five miles long. A pencil stuck into the soil will keep mealy bugs from attacking a plant. Graphite is non-toxic: pencil makers claim you could eat a pencil a day and not get sick. However, breathing it is another matter: the graphite dust that permeated the Thoreau household may have led to the death of several family members, including Henry, who died of tuberculosis at the age of forty-four. Automatic pencils turned up toward the end of the century, colored pencils in the 1920s.[22]

A California sculptor named Agelio Batle makes clever writing instruments out of pure graphite combined with

22 There are two great pencil tunes that I'm aware of: "Lead Pencil Blues" written by Johnnie Temple in 1935 and recorded by many of the great bluesmen, including Robert Johnson and Muddy Waters, and also Horace Silver's "Pencil-Packin' Papa" on his eponymous 1994 album.

"smudge-resistant compounds." They are clean and lustrous, pleasant to write with and great fun to draw with, and beautiful objects in themselves. Among Batle's creations are a cast of his own hand (index finger pointing), a grasshopper, a magnolia bud, a gingko leaf, and a pepper—but the most whimsical is a graphite quill. Writing with this combination of the quaint and the practical almost elevates even the most humble penciled scribble ("buy onions") to the level of art.

Spencerian Alphabet

Aa Bb Cc Dd Ee

Ff Gg Hh Ii Jj

Kk Ll Mm Nn Oo

Pp Qq Rr Ss Tt

Uu Vv Ww Xx Yy Zz

Chapter Two

The Golden Age of Penmanship

SPENCERIAN SCRIPT

It was during the quill era that Platt Rogers Spencer devised his philosophy of penmanship. The "father of American handwriting" was born in 1800 on the Hudson River, but spent his youth first in Greene County in the Catskills, then (after a fifty-two day trip in a covered wagon) on what was at that time the frontier: Ashtabula, Ohio, in the Western Reserve.

He was the youngest son of a widowed mother who encouraged in her ten children a love of learning—a love that young Platt took to his own extreme. Even at an early age, he was crazy about handwriting but, in a family too poor to provide him with paper, he was forced to practice on leaves and bark, in the snow, and on the sandy beach of Lake Erie, where sometimes his obsessive script would stretch for half a mile. Finally, when he was seven, he got hold of some paper to write on and never looked back: he blossomed into an excellent junior penman—and the kind of remarkable child who inspired heroic tales: He once walked twenty miles, barefoot, to borrow a book, with only raw turnips to eat on his journey.[1]

Platt Rogers Spencer

1 He was an equally unusual adult: once, having no paper or pen, he demonstrated his script for a visitor with a broomstraw and the blood from his finger.

Spencer was a mere fifteen when he began teaching handwriting to others—probably the ubiquitous copperplate—and so intense was his zeal that he sometimes forgot to collect payment from his students. He was also an intensely moral young man, and would have liked to become a minister, but a period of alcoholism convinced him that a religious career was not the path for him. As was the case with many great men, though, his fall was followed by redemption: in an effort of will, he gave up drinking in 1832 ("I hereby pledge to God and the world that I will never taste another drop of liquor"). He became a lifelong teetotaler and a vigorous advocate of the benefits of swearing off, and in a poem from 1837 he advised young people to "Touch not the juice that woos the taste."

Spencer's sweetness and tenderness of heart were often mentioned by his family and his students. He was a gentle soul who loved to sing, and, according to one of his pupils, he filled his schoolrooms with "sunshine, life and song." President James Garfield, when he was still a congressman, first met Spencer at a lecture in Ohio in 1857, and the two struck up a friendship—united by, among other things, their staunch opposition to slavery. After Spencer's death, Garfield called him "a gifted, noble, and true-hearted man" and noted the admirable fact that "at a time when sympathy with the slave meant not only political but social ostracism, Mr. Spencer was outspoken in his denunciation of slavery in all its forms." As for Spencerian script, Garfield called it "the pride of our country and the model of our schools."

Spencer worshiped poetry, and had a vast stock of it—some his own—stored in his memory. But instead of becoming a poet, as seemed likely, he relegated the art to a sideline and, demonstrating a highly unpoetical practical streak, became a professional penman and teacher. He founded a chain of business schools (which, at a time when there were less than a hundred public high schools in the entire country, actually functioned as private secondary schools), beginning with the Spencerian Commercial College in Pittsburgh, where penmanship was a vital part of the curriculum along with accounting, book-keeping, and business law.

In 1828, Spencer married a woman with the marvelously apt name of Persis Duty, who stuck by him through his drinking years: as he put it, she saved him, by her devotion, from "the drunkard's melancholy fate."

She also bore her husband eleven children (the last when she was fifty years old), assisted in the running of his schools, established a free library in Ashtabula County, joined him in speaking out against slavery, and was his enthusiastic hand-maiden in his passion for penmanship.

Persis Duty Spencer

By then, he had perfected his own script. Just as Somerset Maugham couldn't look at a sunset without thinking how he would describe it, Spencer couldn't look at a leaf or a stone without thinking how to turn it into a letter of the alphabet. His script was based on natural forms. To Spencer, the stones washed smooth by the lake became the ovals that are the foundation of his letters; arching tree branches and smooth-flowing streams led him to his graceful connecting lines. Remembering the joys of nature—the wild flowers, the smooth pebbles, the beams of sunlight, the flight of birds across a sky traced with wispy clouds—he mingled round and angular, light and dark, trailing vines and curling stems, slender upstrokes and shaded downstrokes, swooping capitals and judicious flourishes.

Spencer's script was meant to be rhythmic and comfortable, a reaction against—though definitely an outgrowth of—the slow, laborious copperplate. Spencer always carried a few pebbles in his pocket—one of the many endearing facts about him—that he would trot out to illustrate the shapes his students should strive for. He also wrote a poem about his inspiration that sums it up nicely, if a tad floridly:

Evolved 'mid Nature's unpruned scenes,
On Erie's wild and woody shore,
The rolling wave, the dancing stream,
The wild-rose haunts in days of yore.
The opal, quartz and ammonite,
Gleaming beneath the wavelet's flow,
Each gave its lesson—how to write—
In the loved years of long ago.

To Spencer, the ideal of the eighteenth-century writing masters—six to twelve hours of practice a day—would have seemed exactly right. In reality, the average pupil didn't have such long hours at his disposal, but an approximation of the script could be learned by any conscientious striver. In the 1840s, a student named Charles N. Hall at the Bridgewater Normal School in Massachusetts (now Bridgewater State College), worked diligently to perfect his penmanship. After pages and pages of drills like this:

young Charles could produce a pretty creditable hand:

Spencer's business colleges, and especially the handwriting philosophy they espoused, were an enormous success. Spencerian script became the official hand of government clerks,[2] and even the lowliest handwriter aimed at some species of Spenceresque elegance. Today, the Spencerian school slogan, "Education for Real Life," may seem singularly unrealistic. Spencerian script, to our modern eyes, isn't much easier or plainer than its predecessors, and has little to do with a real life that is usually rushed and fragmented—probably no less a century and a half ago than it is today.

But there were degrees of "fanciness." The "business" Spencerian hand could be markedly faster and less ornate than the script one might use to copy out a poem or write a love letter. The variations ranged from "running hand" (smaller and with more widely spaced letters than standard Spencerian), which could be rapid indeed, though it is far from plain:

2 His sister was the head of the "ladies' division" of a Spencer school in Washington, D.C., that provided training for government work.

Practice from a nineteenth-century copybook

to the heavily shaded and embellished ornamental versions executed by professional penmen, who were greatly in demand both as teachers and as calligraphers for the creation of invitations, diplomas, calling cards, and legal documents:

Script by the revered penman Francis B.Courtney (1867–1952), a graduate of the Spencerian Business College in Cleveland, Ohio

For half a century, from before the Civil War to the end of the Victorian era, the hegemony of Spencerian was a testament to an appreciation for beauty that lurked in the souls of Americans—an appreciation that was closely tied to upward striving: such an extravagant, impressive, high-class script, such an obvious love of the noble and the beautiful—these were surely the mark of a gentleman or a lady. Spencer taught that, by contemplating—and reproducing—the beauties of nature, the young penman would keep his mind out of the gutter (and himself off the juice) and become a refined person of high moral integrity.

But it was mostly after Spencer's death in 1864 that the empire really took off, turning out a nation of writers who were eager to learn the value of an elegant hand and didn't shy away from the seriousness of the quest. As they learned to train the mind by disciplining the hand (and vice versa), Spencerian aspirants were made to break down the letters of the alphabet into seven "principles":

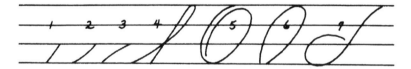

The 1st is a straight line, *the 2nd is a* right curve, *the 3rd is a* left curve, *the 4th is an* extended loop, *the 5th is a* direct oval, or capital *O,* *the 6th is a* reversed oval, *the 7th is the* capital stem.

From these few essential lines, curves, and loops, the letters can be constructed systematically and with proper proportions that have been carefully worked out. Written on lined paper, a capital E, for example, which utilizes principles 2, 3, and 5, is divided into three spaces: the top oval fills the highest space; the bottom oval fills the two lower ones, with a width of a space and a half; the width of the top oval is half that of the lower; the length of the first curve takes up three-quarters of a space; and the length of the smallest loop one-third.

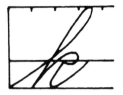

The lower-case k requires four principles (1, 2, 3, and 4), and particular care must be taken to ensure that between its two loops the distance is half a space.

These constructions were built using Spencer's famous "whole-arm movement," which—unlike the hand movements necessary for copperplate script—emphasized bringing the entire arm, from shoulder to fingers, into play when writing.

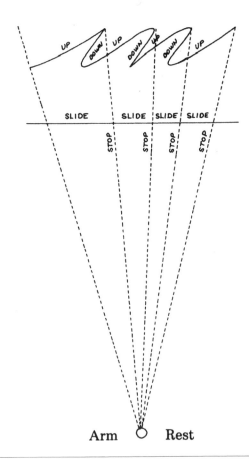

From Theory of the Spencerian System of Practical Penmanship

As Spencer warned in one of his didactic poems:

He who would be a writer, fine,
Must take a deal of pains,
Must criticize his every line,
And mix his ink with brains.

Spencer died, at sixty-three, upon his return from a trip to New York City to give a lecture on his methods at a business college. His last request was for his pen, and he died with it clutched in his hand. The pen might well have been one of the new metal ones, but on Spencer's seven-foot-high tombstone (in Evergreen Cemetery in Geneva, Ohio, nine miles from Ashtabula) is carved his famous signature and under it a magnificent goose-quill pen, three feet long—the instrument with which he began his amazing career:

Spencer's tombstone

Spencer's schools continued, run by his siblings, his sons and daughters, and various other relatives. There was some strife among the numerous descendants: his sons apparently tried to shut out his daughters and claim sole credit for the triumph of the Spencerian juggernaut. Sara, his oldest, became a dedicated writing teacher and a renowned penwoman in a world in which most penmen were just that: men. She never forgave the refusal of some of her sisters to do the same.

The schools prospered, however, and turned into a mini-industry, spawning a series of popular textbooks. There were other gifted penmen at the time, teaching their own impressive scripts—Charles Paxton Zaner and Elmer Ward Bloser, in particular, have had a lasting impact on American penmanship. But Spencerian was the basis for the penmanship taught in most public and private schools across America. Anyone who has come across a bill of sale from, say, 1879, or a letter from a great-great-grandmother describing the rancorous Hayes-Tilden election or the ribbon trim on her new muslin bonnet, is probably looking at some approximation of Spencerian script—as in this excerpt from an 1898 letter:

or this page from the "little red book" of home remedies compiled by a woman from the same era:

Catarrh

INSURE WITH THE

Old Hartford Fire Insurance Co.

ORGANIZED 1794

An important part of treatment is a warm *moist* atmosphere

Quick Home Cure for Catarrh:—
1 Teaspoonful Common Salt
1 Teacup of Milk
½ pint warm water.
    Use as injection for nostrils three times a day.
or — Same quantity of
Borax instead of Salt

Catarrh (Nasal).

R̃. Acid Carbolic liq.   30 ℳ
Soda Bicarb.   1 ʒ
Soda Biboras   1 ʒ
Glycerina   ½ ℨ
Aq. Rosæ   3½ ℨ
Mft. To be used with atomizer 4 or 5 times a day.
    (See page 18)

20

Losses Paid $50,000,000
Assets $10,819,629

Snake Bites.
(Rattlesnake, Copperhead, Water-moccasin, Viper)
When upon a limb, tie or twist a band or fillet around the extremity above the wound.
    Several such bands are better.
If on arm, bind above elbow near the shoulder.
If on hand, bind at wrist (above wrist bones).
If below knee, bind above knee.
If on upper part of leg, bind well up near groin.
The Band may be a strap, rope, cord, handkerchief, or anything that can be drawn or tied tightly, — or if tied loosely, will permit of placing a stick within it, and twisting tight.

The Spencerian Key to Practical Penmanship—written by Spencer himself and published by his five sons shortly after his death—remained hugely influential until the twentieth century, when A. N. Palmer and his famous "method" began to make serious inroads.

Spencerian is far from dead. Calligraphers love it: Maureen Vickery, a Houston calligrapher, not only hand-letters a lovely Spencerian script for envelopes, invitations, place cards, etc., but also has a small but thriving sideline teaching it as a "monoline" script that can even be effectively produced with a ballpoint:

> *Beautiful handwriting is of that value which cannot be bought or sold but is obtained by practice and application.*

There are some interesting revivals from time to time—among them this 2007 ad campaign for Saks Fifth Avenue by Marian Bantjes:

The Coca-Cola Company

Spencer's most enduring legacy—and the most visible use of his script today—is the Coca-Cola logo. It was designed in the 1880s by a man named Frank Robinson, a bookkeeper employed by the founder of the company. Robinson may very well have been trained in business and penmanship at a Spencerian school—the logo in his handwriting, while impressive today, was most likely a typical bookkeeper's hand of the time. But whatever the case, it has survived. Most Americans probably see this sterling reminder of Spencer's genius every day of their lives.

But generally, by the turn of the twentieth century, the Spencerian style was becoming as passé as the horsehair bustle. Spencer's elaborate loops and curls, which for most people had to be executed with painstaking care, had become less appealing to a nation that was rapidly swooning into the romance with business and commerce that would dominate it for the rest of the twentieth century and beyond. A 1902 lament in a Zaner-Bloser publication, the *Penman, Artist and Business Educator*, puts it this way: "The young men of today do not exercise the patience which leads to the top in ornate writing, nor have they the time to acquire a style of handwritng for which there is only a limited market in these strenuous times." Even the relatively stripped-down Spencerian script taught in business schools was considered too slow, too nitpicky, possibly even too *feminine* in a culture that worshiped masculine achievement and saw the prospect of women entering the business world—something they were doing increasingly—as a potential threat.[3]

3 Spencer's youngest child, Ellen, tried to enroll at the law school at Georgetown, but was refused because she was female. Being her father's daughter, she studied law on her own and was admitted to the Washington, D.C., bar when she was forty-two.

A B C D E F G H I J K L M
N O P Q R S T U V W X Y Z

a b c d e f g h i j k l m n o p

q r s t u v w x y z 1 2 3 4 5 6 7 8 9 0.

THE PALMER METHOD

A. N. Palmer's patented "method" was designed to be the perfect script for the world of commerce. Palmer was another lover
of letters who wanted nothing more than to simplify penmanship, to transform it into "rapid, plain, unshaded, coarse-pen,
muscular movement writing," as the subtitle of *The Palmer
Method of Business Writing* puts it.

A. N. Palmer

Teddy Roosevelt, the Rough Rider who carried the big
stick, was president of the U.S. (1901–1909) during Palmer's
rise to penmanship prominence. Just as Garfield—himself a
teacher and a penman as well as a lover of poetry and student
of the classics—was the right president for Spencer, Roosevelt
seems emblematic of the Palmer era. Indeed, Teddy's life mir-
rors handwriting's evolution from Spencerian to Palmerian:
he started out as a sickly, delicate, myopic, dandyish young
man who went west, hung out with cowboys, and transformed
himself into a superb, vigorous specimen of masculinity.

Palmer, in his introduction to *The Palmer Method of
Business Writing*, states that it "has not been written to exploit
anyone's skill as a pen artist." Palmer was a great admirer
of Spencerian writing, but in his new, improved script there
would be no curls and swirls, none of this moral uplift stuff,
no wifty meanderings about flowers and sunbeams. America
needed "good, practical business writers," and—by jingo!—his
little red book was going to produce them.

Palmer (1860–1927) was born on a farm in St. Lawrence
County, New York, and, like Spencer, he lost his father when
he was young—Spencer at six, Palmer at thirteen. The wid-
owed Mrs. Palmer moved the family to Manchester, New
Hampshire. There, Palmer enrolled in the Bryant & Stratton
Business College,[4] run by George Gaskell, an admirer of
Spencerian handwriting and the author of the popular book
Gaskell's Complete Compendium of Elegant Writing (1873), which
over the years sold hundreds of thousands of copies. *Gaskell's*

4 Bryant & Stratton was a
major chain of business
colleges; bookkeepers
and accountants, of
course, were expected
to be not only quick with
figures but proficient
with a pen. B&S still
exists, with fifteen
campus locations and
"a contemporary career-
focused format" that
does not, alas, include
penmanship instruction.

Compendium of Forms, Educational, Social, Legal and Commercial was another smash hit, a "complete encyclopedia of reference" that included sample letters (concerned mother to daughter away at school: "I have been somewhat alarmed because your last two letters do not run in that strain of unaffected piety as formerly. What, my dear, is the reason? Does virtue appear unpleasant to you? Are you resolved to embark in the fashionable follies of a gay, unthinking world?"), tips on Street Etiquette ("When a gentleman is escorting a lady..., it is his duty to insist modestly on carrying any article she may have in her hand, except the parasol...; that article must not under such circumstances be borne by the gentleman...."), a Political Dictionary (*Abolitionist* to *Yankee*), a section on The Language of Flowers (apricot blossoms express doubt, marigolds despair), and Maxims of George Washington, including, "In the presence of others sing not to yourself with a humming voice, nor drum with your fingers or feet."

An entrepreneur who believed in the power of advertising, Gaskell was one of the most prominent penmen in America. It was at his school that the young Palmer was introduced to the glories of penmanship, and was such a devotee that (again like Spencer) he became a teacher when he was still a teenager, moving west from New Hampshire to Missouri as an itinerant penman—an occupation that was far from unusual. In 1880, Palmer finally settled in Cedar Rapids, working in an office as a clerk and bookkeeper—his first real job. It was there that Palmer had the revelation that changed his life and the lives of countless American schoolchildren: writing with curls and flourishes was all very well, but in the world of business, speed was all-important. As he watched his colleagues at work, busily scratching out inventory lists and columns of numbers in a brisk utilitarian ad hoc scrawl—probably a severely minimal, unadorned running hand—he realized that the lifted-arm movements necessary to produce gorgeous Spencerian script not only required "a deal of pains," they also required a deal of time. And if you tried to write Spencerian quickly, you'd end up with a sore arm and a nasty scribble.

A clerk or a penman who had to write all day—and was sometimes paid by the word—needed a new method with no superfluous motion, no tiring lifts, arm on the desk, the work done by the hand, wrist, and forearm working together. Thus was fixed in the mind of Austen Palmer the concept of *muscular movement* that would bedevil schoolchildren for nearly a century: "with the larger part of the arm below the elbow on the desk, the fingers not being held rigid, but remaining passive, and neither extended nor contracted in the formation of letters."

The concept of muscular movement was not new—penmen throughout the nineteenth century had used the phrase—but the insistence on forearm and hand movement over fingers was pure Palmer. So too was the notion that handwriting should become automatic, that the muscles of the properly trained writer could do the job and not much mental effort should be required.

Armed, as it were, with a steadfast faith in the value of this daunting calisthenic, Palmer quit his job and went back to teaching. He was just past twenty. By the time he was twenty-eight, he had founded the first American penmanship magazine (*The Western Penman*), published *Palmer's Guide to Muscular Movement Writing*, and mastered, as Gaskell had, the art of advertising, using his own publication to tell the world about the course of instruction he devised.

His ideas caught on. They appealed strongly to the Catholic schools, probably because they emphasized discipline and hard work. In 1904, Palmer demonstrated his Method at the St. Louis Exposition, complete with a collection of persuasive befores and afters—ugly scrawls magically transformed into efficient communications. It took the public schools longer, but a New York City superintendent who saw the exhibit was blown away. Within four years, half the students in the public-school system there (285,605 of them) were toiling away at the Palmer Method.

Easter 1896 issue of The Western Penman

*Palmer Method
Progress Pin,
awarded for
superior hand-
writing*

By 1912, his name was a household word, and a million copies of his textbook had been sold. When he died, at age 66, in 1927, the A. N. Palmer Company was a corporation with offices in New York, Chicago, Cedar Rapids, and Maine—a giant in the education world that, in addition to supplying books and writing utensils, rigorously trained scores of teachers in Palmer's "commercial cursive." More than twenty-five million people had been Palmerized, and the Method was being taught in three-quarters of the schools in America.

Palmer was interested in consistency, legibility, and—especially—speed. It was increasingly true that, as Calvin Coolidge famously put it, "the business of America is business." There wasn't much room in that world for individuality. Palmer paid lip service to the idea: individual variations in the Method were permissible "within certain well-defined boundaries"—and enthusiasts regretfully admitted that individual character was impossible to suppress. But in practice, the entire classroom was supposed to be making their letters in exactly the same way, the same size (lower case was about one-sixteenth of an inch high), and even at the same speed (seventy capital C's per minute). All this probably made good sense at a time when industrialization, the assembly line, and mass production were coming into their own. It was all about control.

Palmer's books, like Spencer's, are full of precise, detailed, rigorous, and supremely tedious drills that seem designed to squeeze to death even the most forceful and artistic handwriting. His famous bedspring ovals, for example, were meant to be done for "at least" five minutes:

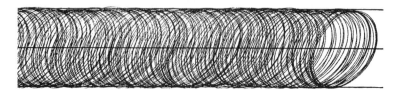

After five minutes of drawing ovals, or up-and-down lines, or

or

or

you'll agree to anything, even to making Palmer's awkward capital *X*—which, contrary to the basic idea of an *X*, doesn't actually cross, but merely *seems* to cross. (To be fair, this was not invented by Palmer: it was the *X* of choice by most penmen going back to the Bickham era. Still, you'd think someone as practical as Palmer would have simplified it.) In Sister Victorine's third grade, getting those swooping curves properly aligned was a frustrating challenge, and it's no easier now.

Then there are his strange capital *Q*'s.[5] At first glance, they look confusingly like the number two. But the 2 form is not as illogical as it seems: it evolved over the years as scribes fiddled with the classic lower-looped Roman *Q*, attempting to turn it into a quicker one-stroke letter:

Palmer capital X

5 Interestingly, the *Q* is believed to be the origin of the question mark, beginning as the word *questio* (Latin: question) at the end of a sentence, which was abbreviated to a *q* over an *o*, which evolved into the simplified doodle-over-dot form that we know today.

Palmer simply took it a step further, so that there is in effect no difference between his *Q* and a normal 2.

In one manual, Palmer cites a lad of twelve who produced three thousand of the bedspring ovals across a page only eight inches wide, "maintaining a uniform speed of two hundred to a minute." He includes tips for students who were not so proficient: if your ovals are too narrow, it might help to repeat over and over (presumably *sotto voce*), "Wider, wider, wider, rounder, rounder, rounder," until you get it. According to Palmer, with half an hour of practice daily, the average student should be able to "lay the foundation for an excellent script" in one school year. But he emphasizes the importance of constant vigilance—not just of letterforms but of posture and movement—if that script is to be maintained.

Some of the illustrations in the Palmer manuals seem designed for Martians unfamiliar with human anatomy. This photograph of a glowering youth demonstrates the proper fingers with which to hold the pen:

Palmer spared no pains in making everything crystal-clear. Like Spencer, he believed that diagrams would help. He recommended "a medium coarse pen" and blue-black ink, and was uncompromising on the role of the right forearm muscles in the production of perfect penmanship. In one of his "To the Teacher" notes, he cautions, "See that pupils' arms are free of heavy clothing," and comments, with approval, "Many good writers consider this of such importance that they cut off the right undersleeve at the elbow."

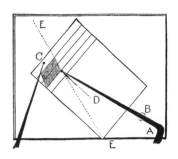

"A *represents the square turn at the right elbow and its position on the desk,* B *is the muscular rest of the forearm,* C *the position of the left hand in its relation to the paper and the right hand,* D *the penholder, and* E-E *the imaginary line between the eyes along which the pen should travel....*"

A class of students demonsrating the above diagram

It's interesting to compare the scripts that have dominated American penmanship over the last 250 years. The flourishes wax and wane, the loops get longer or shorter, and each script seems reflective of its time. Additionally, with the passing of years, each has acquired baggage it didn't have when it was in common use. Copperplate is the iconic image of America's great historical documents. The Spencerian *B* looks to me like the monogram I used to see on my grandmother's towels. Palmer script has a tame, uptight schoolmistressy aura. At their core, though, all these scripts are similar, and all remain readable today:

Ben Franklin's capital B, 1787

Copperplate capital B from a 1797 student copybook

Spencerian B

Palmer Method B

A A B B C C D D
E E F F G G H H I
J K K L L M M
N N O O P P Q Q
R R S S T T U U
V V V W W W
X X Y Y Z Z Y

Copperplate uppercase

a b c d e f f g g h i j k
l m n o p q r s t u v w x
y y z

Copperplate lowercase

Aa Bb Cc Dd Ee
Ff Gg Hh Ii Jj
Kk Ll Mm Nn Oo
Pp Qq Rr Ss Tt
Uu Vv Ww Xx Yy Zz

Spencerian alphabet

A B C D E F G H I J K L M
N O P Q R S T U V W X Y Z
a b c d e f g h i j k l m n o p
q r s t u v w x y z

Palmer alphabet

PALMER AND GENDER

This may be an untenable generalization, but when it comes to handwriting, it seems to me that men have traditionally felt freer to be more creative, or more iconoclastic, or perhaps just messier. They were given more leeway than docile young ladies when it came to producing a careful, readable script. Certain men (the "real-men-don't-eat-quiche" types) consider good handwriting to be a bit sissified, and even today some busy male executives who take pride in their scrawled signatures persist in viewing a legible one as the mark of someone without enough important documents to sign.

But the fact is that the small-motor skills of boys lag behind those of girls, so that in third grade, as we pigtailed darlings were forming our perfect loops and ovals and looking with distaste at the hopeless scrawls of the little boys in our class, we had no idea that they really couldn't help it. And some of them never recovered.

My husband, Ron, effectively demolishes one of my romantic theories. Until I met him, I always assumed artists had "artistic" handwriting, meaning artistic in the conventional sense: beautiful and well-proportioned. But, despite his great-looking signature and his awesome abilities as a painter, Ron has what can only be described as "bad handwriting" that drifts in and out of legibility. It gets the job done, but (to my penmanship-crazed mind) with the finesse of a chainsaw:

The emptiness of Taoism is not the same emptiness as Chan/Zen Buddhism . . .

Ron was an army brat whose family was always moving around the world; he finds my twelve years in the same parochial school as exotic as I do his watercolor lessons in Okinawa. Not only did he lack the fine-motor skills all small boys are deficient in, he also lacked anything resembling continuity in his education. He does, though, remember the Palmer Method exercises he did in his public school in Maine, where his father was briefly based. Ron was especially fond of the bedspring doodles. He saw the Palmer exercises as a challenge, but he approached them more as an artist than as a penman. While I was laboring over my handwriting, trying to make it express the central truth of my inner being, he was scrawling page after page of ovals for the sheer joy of it, as if it were a drawing lesson.

Much earlier in the twentieth century, both my parents were, of course, subjected to Palmer Method in the Catholic schools. My mother was a stellar handwriting student who—maybe because she was forced by her mother to quit and get a job when she was sixteen, putting an end to her hopes of going to college and becoming a Latin teacher—retained an abiding respect for what she learned in school. She stuck closely to Palmer Method, and her handwriting hardly changed from the time she was a young woman until her extreme old age.

One of the biggest events in my mother's life was her elopement to California with my father at the height of the Depression, in the rumble seat of a friend's car. They were married in Joplin, Missouri, by a justice of the peace who gave them a 1921 "Miss Liberty" silver dollar, which I still have— their only wedding gift. They lasted a year in L.A. before homesickness drove them back to Syracuse, flat broke and without winter coats. My dad got a job as a roving PR man for Pepsi Cola[6]—then a fledgling soft drink company—and for nearly ten years he and my mother traveled all over the East Coast, living in hotels. My mother sent regular postcards home to

6 Pepsi too had a lovely Spencerian logo, which persisted until the '50s.

her friend Lee Dusenberry, and Lee saved them all—a colorful record of a memorable time that would lose a lot of its charm if it consisted of printed-out e-mails:

1941

My mother's penmanship was lucid, swift-flowing, expressive. It always looked to me like the rhythmic, vigorous handwriting of a singer, and, in fact, Mom had a strong alto and sang in her church choir until she was well into her eighties. There was a famous incident in the '30s involving a slinky dress, one too many whiskey sours, a grand piano someone hoisted her up on in a Chicago bar, and a rendition of "Moonglow" that brought down the house.

In her widowed old age, year after year, my mother was re-elected secretary of her senior center, possibly because she truly enjoyed taking notes every week and "respectfully submitting" them. Her handwriting never changed much:

Mom, 1935

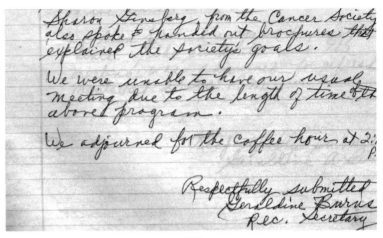

1993

Finally, when Mom was close to ninety and nearly blind, her writing developed a wobble and tended to go uphill instead of marching straight across the page. In her last years, even though we talked on the phone all the time, she still wrote me letters, and she never failed to apologize for her penmanship.

My father had idiosyncratic handwriting that retained an untamed angularity over the course of his short life. (He died in 1957, at the age of forty-six, from rheumatic heart disease.) If my mother was a Palmer Method poster child, my father was a wild 'n' crazy guy:

1955

1943

His handwriting was very much like him: smart, handsome, and rather dashing.

My dad had an artistic side that found its outlet mainly in his cooking[7] and in his meticulous and beautiful architectural drawings—usually of improvements he'd like to make to our house (a workshop, a garage, an attic study), but also of fantastic imaginary buildings, precisely measured out on graph paper. I don't think he ever told anyone about them—maybe no one even knew about them but me (I was a snooper: my parents' bureau drawers and closets drew me like magnets)—and none of them, alas, has survived. But I have a stash of cards and letters written in his quick, spiky script that's as much like him as his image in photographs. If they didn't exist, my world would be a poorer one.

PALMER AND LEFTIES

My two best friends in high school were Eileen and Rosamond, and both were left-handed.

Right-handedness was not forced on the lefties in our school. For years, many left-handers had been persecuted into conformity under the twisted logic that writing with your right hand is easier. (Perhaps inevitably, this has come to be known as the "vast right-hand conspiracy.") If they couldn't adjust they were routinely scolded, ridiculed, dunce-capped, knuckle-rapped, and confined in the coat closet. Neither Spencer nor Palmer even acknowledged the fact that there might be lefties in this world.

But Sisters Victorine et al. were progressive on this point. None of this happened to Rosamond, though she says, nonetheless:

Being left-handed was like having a name like Rosamond.

7 In the '50s, my father cooked eggplant (which no one else I knew had ever heard of), made a wickedly delicious dish of lamb kidneys and heavy cream—unimaginable now!—and, when I had sleepovers, charmed my friends by turning out batch after batch of pancakes shaped like our initials.

Dad, 1940

She goes on, "When I was younger (and very shy) I hated anything that made me unlike all the Marys, Susans, etc. Left-handedness made me even more different, and we all know that survival meant blending in."

Aside from those right-hand inkwells, there are other leftie difficulties Rosamond told me about that wouldn't occur to a "normal" person: your hand smears the ink as you write, note-book binding gets in your way (three-ring binders are a special hell), you have to slant your paper toward the right instead of the left. Receiving change, she says, can be problematic (in a way she can't explain but probably any leftie could sympathize with). If her left-handed scissors aren't handy, she cuts hold-ing the scissors upside down. And as a sort of culmination of all that's difficult about being left-handed, she often has to consciously think which way is left and which way is right—it has never come naturally.

Perhaps astonishingly for a left-hander, Eileen was the acknowledged penmanship goddess at St. John's. She didn't show up until seventh grade. Before that, she was in public school, where, she recalls, in first grade she had to bring from home an official "letter of permission" to the principal (whose name was Miss Wright—I am not making this up) stating that no, it was *not* okay for her teacher to tie Eileen's left hand down so that she'd learn to print the alphabet right-handed. The superintendent of schools got involved, and finally she was grudgingly permitted to be a leftie. Eileen received consistent A's in Handwriting, and, just to spite them all, won a city-wide handwriting contest when she was in fourth grade.

Eileen receives handwriting certificate from the superintendent of schools

Unlike most lefties, who angle the paper to the right, Eileen stubbornly places her paper in "rightie position" and curves her left arm around so that she's actually writing upside-down. The script she produces in this unlikely posture has always been gorgeous and distinctive, a kind of casually florid Palmerized Spencerian that has changed little over the years, except perhaps to become moreso:

—In deep thought on my daily walks, I have recalled much about the 'left-handed / handwriting' issue. Thanks to the sharper memory of my sister, MaryLou, I present the following information / clarification.

The concept of handedness is odd and mysterious. For the survival of the human race, you'd think it would be best if we were all ambidextrous, so that if we lost the use of one hand, we could carry on just as well with the other. So why is an estimated ten to twelve percent of the population left-handed?[8] Despite a lot of research, much of it conflicting, no one seems to have the answer to that.

Left-handers were once considered (at best) severely disturbed or (at worst) agents of Satan. If the Spanish Inquisition found you were left-handed, your chances of being questioned, tortured, and/or exterminated were immensely enhanced. Nearly all languages contain expressions that reflect the ancient prejudice against left-handers. The word *sinister*, with all its evil connotations, is simply the Latin word for *left*; our much more complimentary word *dexterous*, on the other hand, comes from the Latin for *right*. Is it a coincidence that *right* also means *correct*? And it's worth thinking about that there are no left angles, only right ones, no matter which way they turn.

For the record, notable left-handers include Judy Garland, Harry S. Truman, much of the English royal family, Bill Clinton, George H.W. Bush, Barack Obama, John McCain, Osama Bin Laden, the Boston Strangler, Michelangelo (who was left-handed but taught himself to draw with his right), Leonardo da Vinci (in Italian lefties are called *mancini*, literally *crooked*), Marilyn Monroe, Paul Prud'homme (the French have their own insulting word for *left*: *gauche*), Darryl Strawberry, Matt Groening, Bart Simpson, and both Everly Brothers.

8 We are also right- or left-eyed. Make a circle with your thumb and first finger around an object in the distance. Now close one eye, and then the other. The object has become invisible with one of your eyes: if it's the left, you're left-eyed. If you're right-handed but left-eyed (or vice-versa), your "cross dominance" could cause problems, according to some scientists, that include being over-emotional, easily upset, forgetful, angry, and possibly paranoid schizophrenic. But cross-dominance can also help you bat better, hit the golf ball further, shoot more accurately, and recall more trivia.

* * * *

Whether lefties or righties, once our Palmer Method years were over, we indoctrinees went our own ways. Most Americans over the age of thirty-five probably write some version of the Method. I doubt there's anyone left on earth making the Palmer *Q*, but those florid capital *L*'s, for example, have persisted in many people's handwriting. Palmer is like many other skills: it gives you the basics and you run with them. Lots of jazz musicians were trained at Juilliard, and Picasso knew how to draw.

As handwriting instruction waned, the A. N. Palmer Co. fell on hard times and finally went bankrupt in 1987. Today, when handwriting is taught in schools, teachers turn to a variety of systems, most of them Palmer-derived.[9]

9 See Chapter Five.

But handwriting is often simply neglected. Kids learn to print, a few might get some rudimentary Palmer-based cursive, and that's considered enough. Not only is it not thought to be a crucial skill, but teachers now are forced to "teach to the test"—and there is, needless to say, no standardized handwriting test. In the world of incessant testing and "No Child Left Behind," there's scant time for handwriting instruction. For the most part, beautiful penmanship now lives on the planet where people gather around the piano and sing, watch *Gunsmoke* on TV, and go to major-league baseball games in the afternoon: it's the planet of nostalgia.

Chapter Three

Father Michon and My Aunt Fanny

You think you're just making a list or writing a letter, but what you're really doing is drawing a portrait of who you are. *Lettuce, dog biscuits, oatmeal, sour cream*: give it to a graphologist for analysis, and what you'll get back is not a bag of groceries but a look into your psyche—or so says the world of graphology.

No matter what method you were taught, or when you learned it, there's something almost universally irresistible about having your handwriting analyzed—particularly in view of the standardizations the schools have traditionally imposed on our script. While the Palmer Method was tightening its grip on the hands of Americans, handwriting analysis was thriving right alongside it—and cheerfully throwing a monkey wrench into Palmer's beautifully mechanical works. Try though you will to make that lower-case g according to the book, there is room for endless variation in those three or four little strokes. And that's where graphology comes in.

Graphology is the analysis of handwriting with the purpose of revealing personality and character. It's sometimes confused with forensic document evaluation, which, while fascinating, is an entirely different discipline. Forensic specialists are certified by the American Board of Forensic Document Examiners; graphologists, on the other hand, may be part of an organization of like-minded people but there is no board that confers official recognition. And while graphology sees handwriting as a window into the subtleties of personality, the role of forensic experts is more cut and dried: they're brought in when a court of law needs a document authenticated—usually in cases of forgery or to determine whether two documents were written by the same hand.

In the famous Dreyfus case in the late nineteenth century, in which a captain in the French army was wrongly convicted of treason based on a note purported to be in his handwriting, forensic experts never did reach an agreement.[1] Closer to home, Bruno Hauptmann, the kidnapper of the Lindbergh baby in 1932, was convicted and sentenced to death partly through identification of the handwriting on the ransom note. The ransom note in the JonBenét Ramsey murder case was also subjected to forensic analysis—though no helpful conclusion was reached.

For the average law-abiding citizen, however, it's graphology that's intriguing. One thing that makes humans different from other animals is our interest in ourselves. What makes us tick? We love anything that provides clues about who we are—who we really *really* are, deep down in that murky place we call our soul. And, as Tamara Plakins Thornton points out in her excellent *Handwriting in America*, when people turn to any kind of character reading—including handwriting analysis—what they are looking for isn't proof that they're extraordinary, or gifted with genius, or destined for great things. It's a big world: all they really want is an assertion of their individuality, whether the individual revealed is brave or cowardly, outgoing or a loner, highly intelligent or just a

1 Dreyfus was exonerated in 1905, but his conviction and incarceration led to an international scandal, thanks partly to the novelist Emile Zola's famous "J'accuse" letter, published in a Parisian newspaper, which charged the French government with a gross miscarriage of justice.

capable grind. It's fine to be an ordinary Joe, as long as the ordinary Joe is *you*.

The history of handwriting has comprised many distinct styles, but for centuries none of them was about letting the world know that the writer was a unique and creative individual. There are a few early references to this idea: Aristotle commented on the uniqueness of handwriting, the Chinese noted it, a few Romans were mildly intrigued, but among the ancients it went no further. In fact, it was originally considered necessary to sign a legal document before a witness because handwriting could so easily be faked: it was assumed that everyone who could write had an essentially similar script. As Thornton puts it, men and women of early America "regarded handwriting as a form of self-presentation but not self-expression." Differences in hands revealed other things: gender, social class, or occupation. Aside from the how-to manuals of the writing masters, hardly any books were written about any aspect of handwriting at all until the late nineteenth century, when graphology suddenly bloomed, first in France and then in Germany. The idea that each person's handwriting was not only unique but also an indicator of personality traits—the whole notion of self-expression through handwriting—was startling, particularly in conservative scientific circles. But it made sense to a lot of people, and it caught on.

GRAPHOLOGY'S EARLY DAYS

Camillo Baldi, an Italian physician, was the first observer to write about the fact that—like snowflakes, fingerprints, and faces—no two hands are alike. In 1625 he published a pamphlet called *A Method to Recognize the Nature and Quality of a Writer from His Letters.*

Mostly, the work is concerned with literary style, with figures of speech and general tone, and with—bless his heart—spelling and punctuation. But he also included a short, rambling section that's a sort of proto-graphological treatise. He claimed that each person's scribble "preserves a certain quality by which his writing differs from that of others," and he gave a few (somewhat bizarre) examples. Alas, there are no illustrations, but he assures us that "rigidly twisted" characters indicate too much enthusiasm; a regular but rushed script suggests imprudence and lack of judgment; a person shows his age by "brutal..., badly formed" writing. But he didn't explore the concept in any depth, and the idea failed to intrigue anyone but a few random scholars who took it no further.

It didn't begin to catch the public imagination until, 250 years later, a Parisian priest, Abbé Jean-Hyppolyte Michon, seized on it with enthusiasm.

A moralist and reformer, Michon was the first to see handwriting as a wide-open window into the nature of the soul. "The slightest movement of the pen is a vibration of the soul," he claimed, and insisted on the intimate connection between "each sign...which emanates from the human personality, and the soul, which is the substance of that personality." In 1875, Michon coined a word for the study of writing: *graphology*. After studying thousands of samples—many gleaned on his tours of Europe preaching the gospel of graphology to eager audiences—he formulated a code that assigned personality traits to various letter forms, for example, "All weak-willed people cross their *t*'s feebly," whereas "The cheerful cross the *t* with a curved and delicate bar."

Michon was a fascinating and many-faceted man, and a magnetically handsome one—a persuasive preacher whose progressive leanings kept him in constant conflict with the Church. His 1860 treatise advocating a kind of early ecumenicalism was placed on the list of forbidden books known as the Index.[2] He was a noted historian, archaeologist, and botanist— and he was, for forty years, passionately but chastely in love with a woman named Emilie DeVars who, just as chastely,

Abbé Hyppolyte Michon

2 The censorship represented by the Index was in effect until 1966. When I was in high school, I defiantly read *Madame Bovary* and *Les Miserables*, both of which were put on the Index because they were "sensual, libidinous or lascivious"—which of course was one reason I adored them both, although *Peyton Place*, which didn't make it onto the Index, was certainly dirtier than either.

returned his ardor ("a thousand times we were saved when we were aflame with desire") and assisted him with his graphological work. Presumably, neither of them was a feeble *t*-crosser.

A few years later, J. Crépieux-Jamin—an ex-dentist and one of Michon's students—further classified handwriting according to seven quantifiable characteristics: speed, letter shapes, pen pressure, direction (slant), dimension (letter size), continuity (connectors between letters), and organization (the way the writing is laid out on the page). Graphology started to gain momentum. In 1886, the Scientific Congress of the Sorbonne declared it a legitimate science.

At first, the only adherents were European—mostly French and German. One of them was the French psychologist Alfred Binet (1857–1911). He became excited about graphology when he devised an experiment in which Crépieux-Jamin achieved 91.6 percent correctness in differentiating the handwriting of brilliant contemporary philosophers like the historian Ernest Renan and the philosopher Henri Bergson from that of average folks who had accomplished little. Once his own daughters were born, Binet began to focus on the intellectual development of children, and in 1904 was asked by the French government to study the education of retarded children—specifically, to identify which children were in need of special help. Binet tried using graphology to distinguish the intelligent from the slow, but as he explored it further, he was dissatisfied with graphology's lack of scientific rigor, and a bit disheartened that amateurs without graphological training could make correct judgments more than half the time. Binet also tried cranium measurement and palmistry. None of them filled the bill, and what he eventually came up with became the basis for the Stanford-Binet IQ Test.[3]

But despite its disappointments and its failure of proof, Binet took the basics of graphology seriously, as did a Swiss psychologist named Max Pulver (1889–1952), who looked at

3 The Stanford-Binet Test evaluates, among other things, vocabulary, comprehension, pattern analysis, equation building, and memory for digits; it is hotly disputed as to its impartiality and usefulness but is still administered routinely in American schools.

handwriting in terms of three "zones" (the upper zone includes, for example, the letters f, l, and t, as well as i-dots; the middle: a, n, and w; and the lower: g, p, y) and compared them, respectively, to Freud's ego, super-ego, and id—the taller your letters, the bigger your ego; the lower they dip, the more driven you are by your biology.

Klara Roman (1881–1962), a Hungarian psychologist, devoted her professional life to handwriting research. She invented an instrument she called the Graphodyne, which measured handwriting pressure, but she was also among the first to get past Michon's "trait-stroke" approach and look at a handwriting sample in its entirety. Roman's *Handwriting: A Key to Personality*, though dated, is readable and sophisticated, with lots of interesting examples, and many graphologists consider it to be the best book ever written on the subject.

GRAPHOLOGY IN AMERICA

In nineteenth- and early twentieth-century America, graphology—no matter what its emphases—had few enthusiasts. But Edgar Allan Poe was one.

He had no training in graphology or even much knowledge of its existence as a movement, but he had a deep-seated interest in the vagaries of human psychology and the ways they're manifested. When he was appointed literary editor of *Graham's Lady's and Gentleman's Magazine* and began corresponding with writers all over America, Poe became intrigued by the way their scripts mirrored their literary accomplishments. In a series of 1841 essays on the subject (which he himself admitted were written not only to illustrate his belief that "the mental features are indicated...by the hand-writing" but also "to indulge in a little literary gossip"), Poe analyzed—after a fashion—the signatures of dozens of authors.

It's probably no coincidence that the writers he approved of had—in his sometimes eccentric opinion—admirable handwriting, and the ones he considered shams couldn't write their way out of a paper bag. William Cullen Bryant,[4] for instance, is cursed with "one of the most commonplace clerk's hands which we ever encountered..., what mercantile men and professional penmen call a fair hand, but what artists would term an abominable one."

Poor old Ralph Waldo Emerson,[5] who "belongs to a class of gentlemen with whom we have no patience whatever—the mystics for mysticism's sake," writes a "bad, sprawling, illegible and irregular" hand.

On the other hand, in the handwriting of Henry Wadsworth Longfellow[6] (he has "first place among the poets of America"), Poe sees "plain indications of the force, vigor, and glowing richness of his literary style."

4 Bryant (1794–1878), also an abolitionist, lived on Long Island but was a Big Apple booster: it was Bryant who chose Calvert Vaux and William Law Olmstead as the designers of Central Park. He was the author of the surprisingly cheery poem "Thanatopsis," a meditation on death that ends with the image of "one who wraps the drapery of his couch/About him, and lies down to pleasant dreams."

5 Emerson (1803–1882)— Transcendentalist, essayist, poet, radical atheist, and lender of land on Walden Pond to his friend Thoreau on which he built his famous cabin—is now considered one of the great American writers. (In his eulogy at Thoreau's funeral, Emerson approvingly mentioned his friend's pencil-making accomplishments.)

6 When I was in school, we were beaten over the head with Longfellow (1807–1882), who wrote "The Song of Hiawatha"—of which we all remember the lines "By the shores of Giche Gumee, By the shining Big-Sea Water," and not much else. However, one of the poems I memorized was his charming "The Children's Hour," written for his three daughters, which gallops along wonderfully and is really fun to read aloud. Longfellow is now invariably called, rather condescendingly, "one of America's most beloved poets"—also perhaps one of its most unread.

And he says of James Russell Lowell,[7] "entitled, in our opinion, to at least the second or third place among the poets of America," that "the man who writes thus...will never be guilty of metaphorical extravagance, and there will be found terseness as well as strength in all that he does."

But Poe's literary mischievousness hadn't much to do with real graphology, which, like its distant cousin, psychiatry, was slow to migrate to America.[8] Graphology has never been accepted here by the psychiatric community as it is in Europe. Why? The graphologists I talked to ascribed it to Americans' deep-seated puritanism—and hence, close-mindedness. Additionally, American psychologists have tended to view handwriting not as an expression of the deep-seated truths of personality but as merely an aspect of muscle movement that can't be precisely measured and is therefore not worth studying.

In *Handwriting in America*, Thornton attributes its ill repute in this country to an influential experiment done in 1918 by two professors at the University of Wisconsin, Clark R. Hull and Robert B. Montgomery, who were intrigued by Binet's involvement in graphological research. Using the handwriting samples of seventeen medical students, they compared some basic trait-stroke correlations with the students' assessments of each other and found more discrepancy than agreement. Binet's experiments must have been flawed. Graphology was baloney.

Initially, when handwriting analysis made its way to these shores in the early twentieth century, it received a warm welcome. America was moving from an agricultural to an urban society: between 1880 and 1900, the total population of

America's urban areas expanded from eleven to twenty-five million. New York alone grew from a million residents to a million and a half, and Chicago's population doubled. The cities were filling up with farm girls hoping to find respectable work, younger sons with no prospects, displaced persons, adventurers, immigrants, people on the make—the kinds of characters Theodore Dreiser in his novel *The Titan* called "a strange company, earnest, patient, determined…, hungry for something the significance of which, when they had it, they could not even guess."

It was a new world, exciting for many, a wrenching struggle for some, and the people who inhabited it were receptive to new fads, new products, and new ideas that would have aroused only suspicion back in East Beeville: ragtime, peanut butter, the tango, ping pong, canned food—and graphology. A glimpse into the thrilling individuality revealed with every stroke of the pen provided an assurance that, in a city full of strangers, every last stenographer, every line cook and cab driver and factory girl, was important.

One of its first American zealots was Milton N. Bunker, who in 1929 founded a mail-order school grandly christened the American Institute of Grapho-Analysis.

Milton N. Bunker

In his book *What Handwriting Tells You About Yourself, Your Friends, and Famous People* (1939), Bunker waxes lyrical about his young manhood spent tending cattle in Kansas: "long days under the open sky, keeping the shifting herds together" when, "stretched on the springy mattress of the growing grass," he read his first book on graphology.

Bunker's first love, though, was penmanship, and like many a farm boy of his time he dreamed of wielding his pen in a government office. However, no matter how hard he tried ("night after night at the old kitchen table"), he had trouble making his handwriting conform to the copybook models: his lower loops were too long and his letters too widely spaced.

Bunker finally remembered what he'd read about graphology and realized that handwriting was a highly individual matter—and that those individual traits were going to be important in his life.

Bunker became a rigid adherent of the Michon school of graphology. "Every stroke carries a message," he wrote, and claimed that, if he saw a relationship a thousand times, it was valid. He had no qualms about turning this concept into the most blatantly simplistic symbolism: for example, if your handwriting is riddled with "acquisitive hooks"—like that of the notorious bank robber Roy Gardner—you're dishonest, eager to get your hooks into what's not yours. (Other graphologists say that hooks can simply indicate tenaciousness. Gardner's hooks could also be seen as fancy remnants of a Spencerian he may have learned in school.) "The crimes of the man who wrote this," Bunker claimed, "could have been avoided if someone had analyzed his handwriting in time."

Sincerely yours

Roy Gardner.

Bunker worried a lot about "sex criminals," and urged his readers to be on guard for suspicious handwriting: a blotted, smeared, "muddy" script, thick and heavy with ink, "warns of abnormal sex appetite." He found in the script of FDR ("the man who sold himself to the American voter on four different occasions") evidence of selfishness, "mouthiness," vanity, and weak will. He claimed to be able to distinguish a writer with "a love of sweets and rich gravies" from one who "who prefers simple salads." And he deduced—wrongly—from the writing on the ransom notes that Bruno Hauptmann was not, in fact, the kidnapper of the Lindbergh baby.

Bunker made a stern differentiation between his Grapho-Analysis and "outdated graphology." Grapho-Analysis was "exact and scientific," though he doesn't specify what that claim might mean. "It is to be expected," he wrote, "that some uninformed people are still skeptical."

At certain periods in his life, Bunker dubbed himself "Doctor" and liked to load various scholarly-sounding initials after his name, as well as the assertion that he was "an expert in human nature" and "master of seventeen systems of shorthand." He claimed that if he ever published his findings, the lives of many of "the famous of the earth" could be ruined. On the other hand, he also believed that fixing up your handwriting would fix up your character flaws, and his books are full of entertaining case studies of people who were transformed from self-destructive maniacs into solid citizens when they started forming their lower-case *g*'s differently, and losers who became winners when they slanted their script up (optimistically) instead of down (in the dumps). And, by some accounts, he was a shameless plagiarizer of the work of others, including not only safely dead Crépieux-Jamin but his own contemporaries in the field.

They were increasing. Thanks partly to the arrival of refugee graphologists from Europe during the rise of Nazism, the world of graphology was growing rapidly in America. In Germany, where graphology came to be closely associated with psychiatry, the practice that expanded on Michon's simple code became known as Gestalt ("whole") graphology. Gestalt (today also called *holistic*) graphologists take into account not only individual letter strokes but how they connect (or fail to), how they are placed on the page, how they seem to flow—the overall "look" of the handwriting sample. They use some of Michon's trait-stroke correlations, but they temper them with spontaneous intuitive insights, linking up various traits revealed in the writing to form a complete and nuanced picture of an individual. A graphologist I consulted put it this way: "Nothing *means* anything on its own, and one trait can even contradict another. There are no easy equivalents." A person identified as a quick thinker (fluid, rhythmic handwriting) with more than her share of imagination and creativity (tall upper loops, erratic letter joins), but who also uses very light pen pressure (showing timidity) and an extreme rightward slant (possible indicator of emotional problems) might be described, after close graphological scrutiny, as a bright, creative person who has trouble accomplishing anything.

Unsurprisingly, the Gestalt practitioners gave scant respect to Bunker the backward-looking trait-stroke plagiarist. But he thrived nonetheless. A wildly creative marketing genius who could have sold fleas to a dog, Bunker would not have been out of place in a novel by Sinclair Lewis, and he had more than a little in common with the King and the Duke in *Huckleberry Finn*. One of his first money-making brainstorms was an attempt to sell shares in the Institute to his correspondence students. That grandiose idea didn't pay off, but he did get them to pay dues,[9] and managed to turn many of them into a quasi-cult that swore eternal fealty and took a vow not to spend their money on the writings of his competitors.

Bunker was easily graphology's most colorful character, and he and his flamboyant schemes managed to prosper until, in 1950, the Federal Trade Commission issued a cease-and-desist order, and he had to mend his ways. He died in 1961, leaving behind a mixed legacy: he had certainly helped to popularize the idea of handwriting analysis, but he had also, in the eyes of many, seriously set back the cause. Today there is still a struggle between the Bunkerites (who go by the trademarked name *graphoanalysts*) and everyone else in the field—

9 Dues today are $90 a year. There are 6,000 members.

between strict trait-stroke analysis à la Michon, and the looser, more intuitive holistic route espoused by the majority of today's graphological community. As one of the graphologists I interviewed put it, "What a perfect name for someone who specialized in bunk."

Of course, Bunker wasn't the only grapho-opportunist. The field was crowded with practitioners who claimed that, by looking at a person's script, they could predict heart attacks or deduce eye color or divine the sex of an expected baby. But the fact that something is untrue, unsound, and preposterous doesn't mean it won't appeal to vast numbers of the American public.[10] The early twentieth century was the heyday of do-it-yourself graphology books, cheap pamphlets, and avidly read newspaper columns with pop graphological insights, of vaudeville performers who combined handwriting analysis with phrenology and crystal balls, of con artists who promised to increase your income by digging out the secrets of your script, and of enterprising practitioners advertising their services on the backs of cereal cartons and soap boxes.

10 "No one ever went broke underestimating the intelligence of the American public," according to H. L. Mencken. As part of the American public, I've always thought that was a bit unwarranted, but, on the other hand, 12 percent of Americans today are apparently convinced that Joan of Arc was Noah's wife.

EXPERIMENTS IN GRAPHOLOGY

Interestingly, two of the early graphologists in America, and among the most influential ones, were women: Louise Rice and June E. Downey.

Louise Rice (1874–1959) was an even earlier supporter of graphology than Bunker, and she was probably the most famous practitioner, known to thousands as the author of a popular handwriting analysis column that appeared in a variety of periodicals from the New York *Evening Telegram* to *Movieland* magazine.

An odd mix of serious adept and dogged self-promoter, Rice was a strongly feminist woman who wrote cookbooks, pulp-magazine stories, and potboilers. She also worked as a newspaper reporter, and discovered graphology while she was on assignment in Europe. She not only perfected the art of handwriting analysis herself but taught it to countless others. (Bunker, in fact, was one of her students, but the two ended up on opposite sides of the graphological fence, though Rice was one of the writers he later plagiarized.)

Rice had the sincere idea that graphology could help people with their psychological problems. "Are you happy?" she asked in one of her ads. "If not, why not? Are your wishes well suited to your possibilities? Your handwriting tells me your individual powers of popularity and success!"

Rice's analysis of George Gershwin's handwriting is in the archives of the Theater Division of the New York Public Library; it was commissioned as part of the research material for Clifford Odets's screenplay (other writers were later brought in) for the 1945 biopic *Rhapsody in Blue*.[11] In a letter to Odets, Rice wrote: "If [Gershwin] had not had his music he might have become really dangerous to himself and others..., what psychologists call a 'split personality'....I have never had such a difficult set of handwritings to analyze as this man was such a complex person."

Her book *Character Reading from Handwriting* (published in 1927 and still in print) is a period piece indeed. The bulk of the book is a detailed instruction in basic handwriting analysis— long descenders, for example, indicate the physical and moral courage of someone who "is well able to fight his way through the world"—but she doesn't stop there. She also includes sixty-five pages on the history of handwriting, a chapter (more benign than it sounds) called "Racial and Other Indications in Handwriting," another one on "Familiar Signs" (which begins informatively, "The so-called Roman Numerals are neither Roman nor numerals"), and an extensive section in which she classifies humanity into eight types, including the Material Type (tactless, heavy-set, prone to heart disease, but "a good wife or husband to a mate who is not too exacting"), the

11 Rice charged Odets $20 for her analysis, but added, "If the studio is paying for it, I will leave the price up to you as you know what the traffic will stand better than I do."

Nervous Type (often light-haired, often criminal, often well-dressed), and my personal favorite, the Mental Type (bad at sports but possessed of "a subtle charm": "the women of this type have...made a very distinct advance over their brothers in the field of the novel and in the field of fiction generally"). The handwriting of the Mental Type is pretty inclusive: it can exhibit "the heavy pressure of the true Materialist" or "the light pressure and irregularity of Nervous formations"; the small *g* can be "like the figure 8" or "with the loop all but eliminated." But it's "almost invariably" very small, with wide margins.

Compared with Louise Rice, June Etta Downey (1875–1932) was more credentialed and certainly more focused. Downey was a respected academic who dabbled in neither cooking nor celebrity handwriting. Born into a prominent Laramie pioneer family, she was the sister of a U.S. senator, the niece of a famous mountain climber, and the daughter of a territorial administrator who founded the University of Wyoming. She graduated from Wyoming (majoring in Greek and Latin), went to Chicago for her M.A. and Ph.D., and then returned home to teach at the university—first English and philosophy, then the relatively new discipline of psychology.

June Etta Downey

Professor Downey—a greatly beloved teacher who also wrote the UW alma mater—began her researches with a strong belief in the validity of handwriting analysis—her dissertation had been titled "Control Processes in Modified Handwriting: An Experimental Study." She was intrigued by all aspects of motor behavior and by the mind-body connection. The main focus of her graphological studies was the *process* of writing, i.e., muscular movement, rather than the writing itself, and her graphological researches ultimately disappointed her. She found little evidence to support most trait-stroke claims (e.g., upward slants equal optimism), and wrote that a graphologist could "compare varying details with most painful exactness and yet totally miss the graphic pattern." She championed a less "mechanical" analytic procedure—a holistic outlook—but even then was cautious because of the absence of controlled experiments.

However, while she was still a believer, she created a test known as the Downey Individual Will-Temperament Test, one of the first studies to evaluate character rather than intelligence. Her assertion that it was not useful to separate a single attribute, like intelligence, from the personality as a whole was a departure from the work of Binet and other psychologists of the day. The test employed not only graphological principles but an analysis—called a "muscle reading"—of the subjects' movements in order to compile statistics about "will-temperament," the term Downey devised for "volition." Using the results, Downey—like Louise Rice—classified people into basic personality types, this time an economical three of them: the Hair-Trigger (Impulsive) Type, the Willful (Decisive) Type, and the Accurate (Careful) Type.

Downey's interest in the somewhat vague field of "temperament testing" also encompassed the outright craziness of the Fernald Achievement Capacity Test, which was based on the idea that the longer a person can stand with his heels exactly one-quarter inch off the floor, the stronger his drive and determination; it was hoped that the test might separate young men of staunch moral fiber from budding delinquents.[12]

12 One problem with the test was the difficulty of monitoring subjects to make sure they were elevated precisely one-quarter of an inch—picture graduate students creeping around on the floor with tiny rulers.

The times must have been ripe for offbeat psychological theories—this was the heyday not only of silly pseudosciences like phrenology (reading character from bumps on the head), physiognomy (reading character from facial features), mesmerism, and its outgrowth, hypnotism, but dangerous ones like eugenics.

One of the most interesting studies in graphology was done by Gordon Allport and Philip E. Vernon at the Harvard Psychological Clinic in 1930.

Allport was an Indiana boy, a Harvard hotshot (B.A., Ph.D., professorship, department head), and a "firm believer in the integrity of every human life," which led him to work with troubled youth in Boston. Possibly the most famous story about Allport was his meeting with Freud when he was twenty-two. When Allport arrived at Freud's office, Freud didn't say a word, just sat there waiting for Allport to speak. Finally, flustered, he told Freud that on his way there on the bus he'd sat behind a little boy who seemed to have an extreme dirt phobia: he refused to sit in a seat that had just been vacated by a filthy old man. Freud finally spoke: "And was that little boy you?" Thus began Allport's distrust of psychoanalysis.

Gordon Allport

Vernon was British—he was born in Oxford, but all his degrees were from Cambridge, and his dissertation was on "the psychology of music appreciation," which sounds potentially fascinating but apparently remained unpursued. He met Allport during a postdoctoral fellowship at Harvard, when both were working on the study of expressive movement.

Philip E. Vernon

Allport and Vernon based their research on the idea that people's movements and gestures correlate to their attitudes and values—i.e., their character—and that the way they write is "intricately woven with the deep-lying determinants of conduct." They were especially impressed by the fact that, whether one writes left-handed, right-handed, with the feet, or with a pen held between the teeth, the handwriting is consistent, and that the only factors that could change it substantially would be multiple-personality disorders (in which each "face of Eve" writes differently),[13] extreme drunkenness, or a delusion in which, for example, a patient thinks he's Napoleon and therefore will write like Napoleon.

Allport and Vernon's study—unusually among American scientists—was graphology-friendly. The persistence of particular characteristics in the script of any individual led them to trust it as a tool in understanding personality, but

13 In the movie *The Three Faces of Eve*—for which Joanne Woodward won a well-deserved Oscar for her portrayal of mousy Eve White, slutty Eve Black, and sublimely well-adjusted Jane—the first indication of Eve's split personality comes when her adult handwriting suddenly changes to that of a disturbed child.

they were cautious about the kind of graphology that sees a hook on a letter as the sign of a thief. As they wrote in their book *Studies in Expressive Movement*: "Many of the more superficial graphologists continue to beguile the public with this method." They came out loudly in favor of the Gestalt school—forest, not trees—and quote Crépieux-Jamin's analogy with approval: "The study of details of script is to graphology as the study of the alphabet is to the reading of prose."

An interesting feature of their work was the speculation that—because handwriting does arise directly out of physical movement—the traits a graphologist can pick out most reliably are those with "clearly marked motor concomitants." Looking at indications of speed or slowness, or at the pressure of the pen on the paper, a graphologist might see qualities like self-confidence (rapidity) or athleticism (heavy pressure). In addition, Allport and Vernon felt that a writer's social class and educational level are clearly marked in handwriting, and that much can be deduced accordingly from the aesthetics of the letter formations and their spacing, their originality, and the ease or laboriousness with which they're produced. Like good Gestalt psychologists, they stress the importance of intuition, and grant that some individuals may be supremely gifted in the art of reading personality, able to see aspects of handwriting as pieces of a puzzle that, when put together intelligently, form a convincing picture of a unique human being. Their final take on graphology was a cautious affirmative, with the hope that subsequent studies would illuminate it further.

GRAPHOLOGY TODAY

That torch, however, seems not to have been passed. Graphology is now, as always, widely accepted in Europe (the University of Urbino offers a master's degree) and also in Israel, where not only employers but landlords, kibbutzim, and matchmakers routinely request handwriting samples from applicants. But it is still viewed with suspicion by the scientific and legal communities in English-speaking countries. According to a 1997 article in the *Washington University Law Quarterly*, "American courts have traditionally expressed hostility to graphology. Indeed, testimony based on graphology is inadmissible virtually everywhere....[H]andwriting experts and graphologists in general have enjoyed a very low status in the courts. The general and usually well-justified feeling has been that their findings are largely intuitive and that consequently there are often as many opinions as there are experts in the case"—and nothing has happened since to change that perception. The British Psychological Society ranks graphology alongside astrology: both possess "zero validity" in determining personality. The Encyclopedia Britannica flatly calls it a pseudoscience. In *The Skeptic's Dictionary*, California philosophy prof Robert Todd Carroll writes, "Since there is no useful theory as to how graphology might work, it is not surprising that there is no empirical evidence that any graphological characteristics significantly correlate with any interesting personality trait."

Although it has never received the seal of scientific approval, graphology has managed to transcend its shady past and become an underground popular success, viewed positively by a large swath of the public. It's used by countless corporations as a hiring tool, despite the fact that there is no proven correlation between handwriting and job performance. From 1980 to 1995, when it was discontinued because of lack of enrollment, there was even a Psychology of Handwriting program at New York City's highly respected New School of Social Research (now called The New School). Graphologists are a staple of high-school graduation festivities, office parties, celebrity events, and conventions, where long lines are evidence of their popularity. Hundreds of graphologists have a presence on the Internet; they range from serious, scholarly practitioners to a woman who offers a smorgasbord of angel readings, ghost-busting, spells, feng shui, hypnosis, and grapho-therapy exercises that can improve your golf swing.

In 1957, there seemed to be a moment of validation for handwriting analysis. Dr. James A. Brussel, a psychiatrist with an interest in the subject, was consulted in the case of the Mad Bomber, who had planted as many as thirty-seven bombs (injuring several people) around New York City. He wrote a series of notes—most of them lambasting Con Edison ("CON EDISON CROOKS, THIS IS FOR YOU")—to the police and to various newspapers. From them, Brussel deduced—from a combination of factors that included the bomber's handwriting, his choice of words, and plain old common sense—that the bomber was a clean-shaven, well-educated, middle-aged, paranoid, unmarried, foreign-born male who would be wearing a double-breasted suit, buttoned—all true.[14] In the end, however, the arrest had nothing to do with Brussel's assessment. The Mad Bomber was identified by a woman going through Con Ed's archive of employee records: a man named George Metesky, who had been fired in 1931, had written a series of outraged letters to the company, echoing some of the threats in the Mad Bomber's notes. Metesky was found in Waterbury, Connecticut, and immediately confessed to his crimes. He was declared unfit to stand trial because of insanity, and sent to an asylum.

In approaching anything as widely accepted but scientifically unproven as graphology, scientists and skeptics point to the "Barnum Effect," named after P.T. "There's a sucker born every minute" Barnum. (Unfortunately, Barnum never actually said this.) The phenomenon is also known as the Forer Effect, after the psychologist Bertram R. Forer. What it means is that if an astrologer or a tea-leaf reader or a

14 Brussel also claimed that Metesky didn't have much of a sex life as evidenced by the rounded bottoms on his W's, which resembled female breasts—this also seemed to be true. But in retrospect, as Malcolm Gladwell pointed out in an article on criminal profiling in *The New Yorker* (November 12, 2007), Brussel's miraculous feat might have been exaggerated: "He seems to have understood only that, if you make a great number of predictions, the ones that were wrong will soon be forgotten, and the ones that turn out to be true will make you famous."

George Metesky, the Mad Bomber

rumpologist[15] tells you that you haven't fulfilled your true potential, that you often tend to be worried and anxious, that there's an event from your childhood that still haunts you, and that you're sometimes dissatisfied with your line of work, you may very well be impressed with the aptness of the findings. (This is also known as "the Aunt Fanny Effect," meaning, "This could apply to you, me, or my Aunt Fanny!") In 1948, Forer initiated a series of experiments in which, after his students filled out a personality questionnaire, he gave each one this kind of vague, general, platitudinous analysis. Nearly the entire class found the assessments to be astonishingly accurate.

Some critics point out that handwriting analysis bears the marks of the "sympathetic magic" that forms the basis of many ancient beliefs. If you stuck a pin into a voodoo doll, the person it represented would feel the pain. A bronchiomancer could divine the will of the gods from the pattern made by a set of llama lungs hurled against a flat rock. Astrologers saw a pattern of stars that looked like a bull and declared that anyone born when those stars were at a certain point in the sky would have a bull-like disposition— that is, he or she would be obstinate and willful.

Similarly, graphology does rely, to some extent, on the assumption that handwriting is a visual metaphor for human character: an upward-swooping final stroke on your letters means a big heart, a large capital *I* means a big ego, and a fat lower loop on your *g*'s means a big sex drive.

But as Professor Downey wrote, "One may indeed be exceedingly skeptical and yet unwilling to dismiss the whole matter on the ground that graphology is on a par with palmistry, phrenology, or astrology." There's a better case to be made for graphology than for other pseudosciences, and graphologists are quick to make it: the stars are millions of light-years away, but our handwriting does emanate from our

15 An "ancient art" revived by, among others (though not many), Jacqueline Stallone, mother of Sylvester: send her a photo of your naked butt (at least 800 pixels, please), and she will tell you who you are. (Hint: the left side reveals your past, the right side your future.)

brains. In fact, graphologists routinely use the term "brain-writing," a phrase that replaced Abbé Michon's "soul connection" around 1895, and by which they mean that what we write is directly governed by neurological patterns that travel from the brain to the hand and guide the pen, and that these link up with certain personality traits—the idea that is the ground upon which handwriting analysis stands.

Despite the efforts of Allport and Vernon, Downey and Rice, the brain-hand-ink connection may never have been proved in the laboratory to everyone's satisfaction, but we sense that it is true: it stands to reason—we feel it in our bones—that if each person's handwriting is absolutely unique, it therefore must reveal that person's individual nature. Right?

APPLIED GRAPHOLOGY

I thought it would be instructive to have graphologists analyze the handwriting of three people I know well. I was curious to know what objective professionals would have to say about my friends, but mostly I was curious to see if they would agree with each other, and if they'd get things right.

I found three practicing graphologists who were willing to give me some of their time. Tricia Sabol, from Raleigh, North Carolina, has a law degree from Harvard and is a non-denominational ordained minister. She tells me, "I have not done extensive research into why the principles are what they are—I just learned them, and I apply them." She adds:

> I didn't originally set out to make a career as a handwriting analyst. I myself had strong doubts about whether or not graphology is valid, but I still pursued it because I thought it would be a cool thing to do. Very rarely do I have someone come back and say that I was totally off base with an analysis. So I still don't know if it's valid, but my clients really seem to enjoy it, and I enjoy it as well, and those are the things that matter most to me.

Ralph Zackheim, who lives in Oakland, California, turned to graphology back in the '80s after an ordeal with the Housemate from Hell. Wondering if there might be some shortcut that would help him discover in advance—before the midnight weeping sessions—who might be a disaster and who would be easy to live with, he took a series of courses and seminars from Ted Widmer—in northern California he's "the legendary Ted Widmer"[16]—and thought it all made sense. By then, Ralph had had a raise and no longer needed a housemate, but he pursued graphology because it combined the psychological principles he was comfortable with (he's the son of a psychologist and a doctor) with his own intuitions about people. Along with a friend from the class, he began doing handwriting interpretation (his preferred term) at parties and other events. By now, he says he's done several thousand interpretations, and he finds that they have a high degree of validity.

16 Widmer, who died in 2006, was the author of several books, including one with the wonderful title *Crime and Penmanship*, about forensic graphology.

Diana Hall lives in the San Francisco Bay area and makes her living as a graphologist and forensic document examiner, with a part-time "day job" in the medical field. She's chair of the Graphological Society of San Francisco and assistant director of the International School of Handwriting Sciences (a home study course). Like many, she got her start in graphology when she took Ted Widmer's course. Then she stepped in when he needed a secretary, apprenticed with him for a couple of years, and worked with him in partnership for another twelve. When Widmer retired, she inherited his client list. For Diana, graphology is based on her "inner computer," which looks at a writing sample and checks it against everything she has learned. But she says a good graphologist also has to have "a solid grasp of psychology, culture, sociology, etc.—in other words an understanding of people."

The graphologists I talked to don't know why the symbolism of one's handwriting is an unconscious projection of the inner self, or exactly how it can reveal introversion or ambition or family problems. They can't really explain it, either physiologically or psychologically. They're not aware of any research that would refute the skeptics. And none of them cares. All Diana and Tricia and Ralph know is that it seems to work.

The three graphologists requested that the writing samples be written ad lib, "from the heart," not copied from a book or memorized. Although this seemed dubious, I let the graphologists call the shots, but my lab-rat friends did feel that some of their writing was personal enough to provide a few clues. One took the opportunity to wax nostalgic about growing up in New Hampshire, which immediately typed him as a reflective person of a certain age.

> way of life. Everyone we knew in our neighborhood had an icebox. Electric refrigerators would not become commonplace until sometime in the 1950s. Huge cakes of ice would be delivered by the iceman in his vintage 1930s Ford pickup truck. He wore a unique leather piece over one shoulder, and he would grip one of those big pieces of ice with a pair of enormous ice tongs, sling it over his shoulder and bring it in the house and deposit it in the icebox. He knew if we needed ice that

Another's short homey notes about her zinnia seedlings also included lingonberry martinis with her husband and a smoked-pork dinner she was making for a crowd—all indicating a rather upscale, sophisticated life.

> I'm sorely tempted to bring you a lingonberry martini when I come — They are so delicious!

Each volunteer was required to close with a signature, which, because it's seen by others, represents the way a person wishes to be perceived. If it's similar to the rest of the writing, it indicates a healthy and balanced self-image—but often it's radically different.[17] So it's important in any handwriting analysis. But people's names can also disclose their gender to the graphologist.

17 Poe, in his early musings on writers' signatures, was not aware of this distinction.

I sent my samples to Tricia, Diana, and Ralph, and all three returned them with extensive and thoughtful commentary. And, even as my guinea pigs and I tried to keep our skepticism pumped up, and the Forer Effect in mind, we were often impressed with the accuracy of the analyses—though there were some caveats, too. We went over the comments pretty much line by line, and rated each insight. The average was 65 percent on target, 12 percent dead wrong, and 23 percent Aunt Fanny.

It seemed unfair to subject my three friends to scrutiny without going under the graphological knife myself, so I dug out samples of my handwriting from age ten to very recently and passed them on to my panel of experts.

My handwriting through the ages reveals me to be empathic, intuitive, and understanding of others—something I fervently hope is true—as well as ambitious, persistent, occasionally sarcastic (this is all about the way I cross my *t*'s), and slightly impatient (*moi?*). But dang it, at least I'm open to new ideas and tolerant of others' views! I have the doggish (my dog Fanny?) qualities of loyalty and dependability as well as the catty ones of mild introversion and the frequent need to be alone. I don't like to waste time and don't like delay, and I have strong powers of concentration, with the ability "to focus exclusively on a task and exclude all distracting influences." My graphologists did get a few things backward: I wasn't more outgoing as a child than I am now—far from it. The shyness, like the good penmanship, has mostly vanished. Still, though

Aunt Fanny again made a few cameo appearances, I was impressed with the accuracy of the self-portrait that crept into my handwriting. I'd have to agree with my guinea pigs and say the graphologists' observations were right about two thirds of the time.

So where does that leave us? Graphology has no scientific validity—according to the skeptics, these scores aren't much better than those of an untrained observer; Binet recorded approximately the same percentages in 1906—and yet my small sample of volunteers was impressed with the findings. It has a much higher efficacy rate than, say, prayer, which in a $2.4 million study (funded by the U.S. government) at the Mayo Clinic in 2001 was found to have zero effect on death rates, heart attacks, and strokes in more than 1,800 heart bypass surgery patients. And it's way better than my own secret formula for betting on the Kentucky Derby (not to be disclosed here), which works less than 10 percent of the time.

Graphology, of course, depends on the existence of handwriting for its survival. Not much can be inferred from the way we type, give or take a few grammatical errors and Freudian slips—at least not yet. Maybe, as the keyboard takes over our lives, some modern-day Abbé Michon will devise a way of reading character through our choice of fonts and use of emoticons.

Until then, my husband thinks someone should do personality readings from the things people stick up on their refrigerators with magnets. In our own case, the town dump schedule, the library hours, the vet's phone number, and our basic Margarita recipe pretty much say it all.

Chapter Four

Writing by Hand
in a Digital Age

It's interesting how the vocabulary of writing in ink with a
pen on paper persists. Just as we say we send someone a "carbon copy" or "dial" a phone number (or, even more weirdly, use
a "dial-up" computer connection), people still "turn over a
new leaf" and try to avoid a "blot" on their record. Books continue to be "penned by" their authors.

We talk about "blank slates," even though the only remaining tabula rasa (technically, "scraped slate") may be the
name of the round of pizza dough you can buy at Trader Joe's.
We still quote Omar Khayaam: "The moving finger writes and
having writ, moves on." And we keep insisting that the pen is
mightier than the sword, even though the sword was long ago
beaten into computer parts.

But I am not alone in believing (at the risk of sounding
like Platt Rogers Spencer ambling along the lakeshore with
his pointed stick) that the aesthetic appeal of good handwriting is something we should not cease to value. A lot of people are sick of making excuses for their own handwriting, and
even sicker of struggling to read the writing of others. Many

parents would be delighted if their son or daughter left high school not only typing up a storm but writing a fluent, pleasing script. Receiving a handwritten note remains a small but definite pleasure. Even seeing attractive writing on a dental-appointment reminder card or a Post-It or—dare I say it?—a prescription pad is a nice moment in the day.

I'm aware that it's not for everyone. People who grind their teeth in exasperation at the very idea will ask: What's all the fuss about? Give doctors computers! Write slower when you need legibility! What's wrong with block printing? Illegible signatures are harder to forge! Leave the damn kids alone, they've got enough problems without learning some obsolete fancy-schmancy writing! Who cares about a bunch of effete sixteenth-century Italians? Elitist! Time-wasting! Silly!

For the rest of us, the fact that handwriting does hang on—despite everything—seems hopeful and comforting.

There are plenty of diehard scriptomaniacs out there, and—whether they defend the Palmer Method to the death or crave a signature like the first Queen Elizabeth's

A modern interpretation of the signature
of Elizabeth I

or just enjoy curling up with a diary and a fountain pen and hoping for the best—this chapter is for them, bless their ink-stained hearts.

MANUSCRIPTS

At my school, we learned touch-typing in twelfth grade from Sister Joseph Paul (fondly known as "J.P."), who was tall and intimidating, stood for no nonsense, and made us type to music.[1] While "Stars and Stripes Forever" and the Schubert "March Militaire" rattled the windows of the typing room, we hammered out *j-u-j-space* and *f-r-f-space* until we could do it in our sleep (and, being teenagers, we often did). I'm not particularly manually adroit, but I got perfect grades in typing, a feat I ascribe partly to J.P.'s coaching, partly to my years of bad but determined piano playing, and partly to my ambition to become a writer. Even in those days, I knew that required typing.

I was wrong, though. There are writers who persist in writing their books in longhand, rejecting the computer and even the typewriter for various idiosyncratic reasons.

Mary Gordon remembers "the thrill of the Palmer method" and, according to the *New York Times*, to this day writes with a black-and-gold Waterman fountain pen: "Writing by hand is laborious," she says, "but...it involves flesh, blood, and the thingness of pen and paper, those anchors that remind us that however thoroughly we lose ourselves in the vortex of our invention, we inhabit a corporeal world."

J. K. Rowling has written all her mega-selling Harry Potter books by hand—the first, famously, in a café. (She has also confessed that, when she was making up the names of the characters, she jotted them down on the back of an airplane sick bag.) Once, when she complained on her website that she hadn't been able to find any "normal, lined paper" in Edinburgh ("What is a writer who likes to write longhand supposed to do when she hits her stride and then realises, to her horror, that she has covered every bit of blank paper in her bag?"), she was deluged with paper from her trillions of fans all over the world—from single sheets to a stack of notebooks embossed with her name.

[1] I also signed up for her Gregg Shorthand class, partly to avoid trigonometry and partly to prepare myself for heavy notetaking in college. I never used it—it seemed so dorky—but I have not forgotten it—or rather:

Rowling does eventually type it all into a computer. Many writers work this way, advancing along the winding path from scrawled rough draft to printer-ready copy. Joyce Carol Oates begins "the old-fashioned way," then turns reluctantly to her laptop, as does Toni Morrison (pencil and yellow pad), and the English writers William Boyd ("there is something special about the brain-hand interface") and Martin Amis (longhand for fiction, straight into the computer for non-). John Updike begins with pen and paper because he says he needs to hear his thoughts. Stephen King likes to write in longhand: he was forced to do so when sitting at the computer became painful after he was struck by a car in 1999, and continues to prefer it. But in his book *On Writing*, he says, "The only problem is that…I can't keep up with the lines forming in my head and I get frazzled"[2]—and so he also has a computer.

John Irving, however, doesn't own one of those blasted new-fangled devices. According to an interview with Salon.com, he types up his longhand drafts on an old IBM Selectric (he has six working ones, plus three others as sources of replacement parts). Paul Auster goes him one better: like Mark Twain, whose *Life on the Mississippi* (1883) was the first typewritten manuscript to be submitted to a publisher, Auster uses a manual typewriter.

Auster has typed all his twenty-odd books and screenplays on an Olympia portable that he bought second-hand in 1974. In his book *The Story of My Typewriter*, which features paintings and drawings of the Auster machine by the artist Sam Messer, the author refers to himself as "the last pagan holdout in a world of digital converts," and tells us that in the year 2000 he ordered fifty ribbons for his Olympia, which he hoards, using them until the type is barely legible—and he can only hope they'll last out his writing life.

Even more eccentrically—but understandably—one of my favorite travel writers, Patrick Leigh Fermor, born in

2 In the pre-computer age (1931), Virginia Woolf said something similar as she was finishing *The Waves*: "I reeled across the last ten pages with some moments of such intensity and intoxication that I seemed only to stumble after my own voice." (She also said, "My handwriting is going to the dogs.")

1915, was ninety-two when he decided that his handwriting had deteriorated into illegibility and acquired a typewriter, a 1951 Olivetti.

But Jim Harrison beats them all, writing with a pen in a notebook in a house that, according to the *New York Times* reporter who interviewed him in 2007, "looks like a time capsule from the early 1950s," and which Harrison says, "has absolutely nothing to do with life in our time." Not only no computer, but no trendy typewriting machines, either. He must have a writer's bump like a pistachio nut.

The 1951 Olivetti "Scribe"

Wendell Berry got some flak for his 1987 essay, "Why I Am Not Going to Buy a Computer," in which he revealed that he writes with a pencil or a pen on paper, and that his wife types it up on "a Royal standard typewriter bought new in 1956 and as good now as it was then." He uses this method for many reasons, among them his refusal to support the energy industry any more than he has to (he doesn't own a television, either), his dependence on his wife's editing as she types, and the fact that the two of them simply like working this way: "If you don't have a problem, why pay for a solution?" The flak was, of course, because of the spouse/secretary situation. People called his wife his "energy-saving device" and implied that she could be doing "more meaningful work."[3]

Well, it's true that not every writer is married to a willing typist. Nor do we have the advantages of, say, Bill Clinton, who composed his autobiography in longhand (twenty-two thick notebooks) and had an aide type it up.

For a lucky few writers, there's an additional consideration: book signings, which involve the horrors of not only writer's cramp but the twenty-city tour. Among them are the Canadian Booker Prize–winning writer Margaret Atwood, who is probably asked to sign about eighty kabillion books a year.

Understandably, Atwood finds touring burdensome. As she said in an interview, "As I was whizzing around the United

3 Berry's writing has to get keyed or scanned into a computer at some point in the publishing process. Most contracts include a clause requiring final manuscripts to be submitted in electronic format. *Verbatim* magazine's facetious editorial guidelines go even further: "Under no circumstances will a handwritten MS be read. Instead, it will be roundly ridiculed, unless it is written using the Palmer method, in which case it will be stared at in amazement."

Long Pen™

4 The consensus among
   autograph dealers
   and collectors is that such
   signatures don't constitute
   "real" (i.e., saleable,
   collectible) autographs,
   but I wonder how anyone
   would prove they were
   done long distance.
   LongPen duplicates not
   only the appearance of the
   autograph but the speed
   and pressure the writer used
   to produce it. A forensic
   document examiner would
   be stymied.

States on yet another demented book tour, getting up at four in the morning to catch planes, doing two cities a day, eating the Pringle food object out of the mini-bar at night as I crawled around on the hotel room floor, too tired even to phone room service, I thought, 'There must be a better way of doing this.'"

Up to that point there wasn't, but Atwood devised her own solution: a cyber-object called LongPen™.

Atwood sits at home in Toronto and writes on an electronic tablet that's a bit like Jefferson's "polygraph machine," but perhaps even more like the thingie UPS uses to get our signature verifying delivery. What she writes is conveyed over the Internet to a robotic "arm" that copies it into a book someone has purchased.[4] There's a TV screen attached: Atwood can see her fans, and the fans can see her. To people who object that this is perhaps a tad impersonal/insulting/elitist, Atwood points out that it's handy not only for overburdened authors and the publishers who have to cough up their travel expenses, but for those who may not be well enough to travel, who are afraid to fly, who want to be environmentally correct and not waste jet fuel, who can't accomodate all the bookstores and colleges and groups that want them to appear in person. (Presumably, it also benefits the agoraphobic, the paranoid, and the pathologically shy, as well as writers in the Witness Protection Program.) Instead of jetting over to the Edinburgh International Book Festival in 2007, Norman Mailer LongPenned it (his last book-signing before his death on November 10 of that year), as did Dean Koontz at BookExpo America. The novelists Anita Shreve ("I'd do it again in a heartbeat") and Tracy Chevalier ("Everybody wins!") are advocates. LongPen is now being marketed not only to best-selling writers but to movie stars, sports figures, and other celebs who don't have time to face their fans in the flesh. Shortly before his death, the computer-hating and amusingly crotchety English writer Auberon Waugh (1939–2001) noted, "One can live a happy and fulfilled life without having anything to do with these machines, which grow more unpleasant and threatening every day." It's easy to imagine what he would think of such a gizmo.

As a writer, I have to admit that I'm wedded to my computer. But as a reader, I find it difficult to describe the exact nature of the excitement I feel when I encounter a favorite writer's signature—the real, immediate, spontaneous thing, done with a hand and a pen—or better yet, the original manuscript of some work I love. When I'm on vacation, one of my great treats is to seek out writers' houses. I especially love the Maine home of Sarah Orne Jewett, whose *The Country of the Pointed Firs* (1896) is a charming and intimate chronicle that begins quietly ("There was something about the coast town of Dunnet which made it seem more attractive than other maritime villages of eastern Maine") and continues quietly, and as a re-creation of American country life that, even then, was fast disappearing, it's one of the most delightful books I know.

The manuscript is at Harvard, but at her house in South Berwick bits of Jewett's writing have been preserved, and it was wonderful—to me, at least—to get a glimpse of her vibrant, confident hand.

Jack Kerouac's handwritten diary at the New York Public Library,[5] begun when he was seventeen, is recent enough that it looks like anyone's diary, with its neat, undistinguished handwriting, suitably flourished for the period. And yet, somehow, as we imagine the young, earnest hand that penned it, it's hard not to find it a deeply moving document. Years ago, in England, I remember seeing a George Eliot exhibit at the British Museum that included the manuscript of *Middlemarch*—far and away my favorite Victorian novel. The Berg Collection at the New York Public Library owns—among other wonders—Virginia Woolf's incomparable diaries and many of her letters.

5 On the first page of which—September 21, 1939—he "apologizes" for using pen and ink even though he has "some degree of proficiency in typewriting."

X X 1

The Backward View

last.

At length it was the time of late summer
when the house was cool and damp in the
morning and all the light seemed to come through
green leaves, but at the first step out of doors
the sun always laid a warm hand on my shoulder,
and the clear, high sky seemed to lift quickly
as I looked at it. There was no autumnal
mist on the coast nor any August fog, instead
of these, the sea, the sky, all the long shore
line and the inland hills, with every bush
of bay and every fir-top, gained a deeper
color and a sharper clearness. There was
something shining in the air, than and a
kind of lustre on the water and the pasture
grass, a northern look that, except
at this moment of the year, one must go far
to seek. The sunshine of a northern summer
was coming to its lovely end.

From Sarah Orne Jewett's The Country of the Pointed Firs

The point is that these manuscripts are written with pen and ink on paper. Yes, it's interesting to see Toni Morrison's meticulously penned-in changes to her typescript of "The Art of Fiction," but it's nothing compared to getting a look at, for example, Dickens's endlessly corrected, sublimely messy manuscript of *Our Mutual Friend*—both at the Morgan Library:

All these—and much, much more—are there for the ogling in libraries and museums all over the world.

Even more than a personal possession, a writer's script, with its smears, crossings out, second thoughts, and marginal notes, seems to take the viewer directly into his or her mind. The poet Philip Larkin once said, "All literary manuscripts have two kinds of value: what might be called the magical value and the meaningful value. The magical value is the older and more universal: this is the paper he wrote on, these are the words as he wrote them, emerging for the first time in this particular miraculous combination. The meaningful value is of much more recent origin, and is the degree to which a manuscript helps to enlarge our knowledge and understanding of a writer's life and work." In the words of the poet and former NEA chairman Dana Gioia, "Reading is never more intimate than with script. The hand of the poet reaches out to greet the reader." When you see the manuscript of a work that's important to you, it's difficult not to be very aware of that hand holding the pen and forming the letters—and to feel a bit closer to the mind behind it all.

Now that most writers no longer labor over holograph manuscripts, there will come a time when this kind of magic will be gone. Little that's new will be added to the vast store of manuscripts that have come down to us over the centuries. The shape of the letterforms, the cross-outs, the substitutions, the puzzling illegibilities, the changes of mind and slips of the pen, the color of the ink and the type of paper, the egotistical capital *I*'s and the randy loops on the *g*'s—gone, all of it.[6] Someday the job applications and charge-card receipts of the famous may be all that's preserved in manuscript collections.

And then there's the rather stunning idea that if you can't write cursive, you have a lot of trouble reading it, too. Will my mother's diaries look like Sanskrit to her great-grand-

6 Even handwritten music notation (invented in the tenth century by Guido of Arezzo, a Benedictine monk), which is just as fascinating as handwritten words, and just as varied and individual, is in danger of extinction: notation software for computers has been around for several years.

children? Will it be only a small group of specialists who can make sense of the original handwritten manuscripts of Jim Harrison and Wendell Berry, the heartbreaking letters home from soldiers in the American Civil War, or artifacts like this Christmas note Walt Whitman sent to his publisher in 1879?

Shakespeare reportedly wrote a sequel to *Love's Labors Lost*, entitled *Love's Labors Won*—what if, in 2108, it turns up in a dustbin somewhere in Warwickshire? Will there be any-one around who can decipher it? Who will be the last person to send a handwritten postcard? Who will read it?

In an eloquent lament in the *Oregonian* (January 13, 2008) for the decline of the handwritten letter, Jim Carmin sug-gests: "Perhaps our many creative writing programs should emphasize that one of the important facets of being a writer is to express one's thoughts in the writing of letters, and to remind authors that for history to have a more complete and accurate understanding of their work, the millennia-old tra-dition of letter writing is a good way to do it[7]....Just as there is a 'slow food' movement, to counteract fast food and fast life, perhaps we should begin a slow writing movement, to regain the appreciation of writing letters as an important meditative and historically significant activity, especially to literary studies."

My own advice is: if you get a letter in the mail, save it! Posterity will thank you.

7 There are dozens of pen pal organizations, some of which still encourage handwritten, snail-mailed letters even in the age of e-mail.

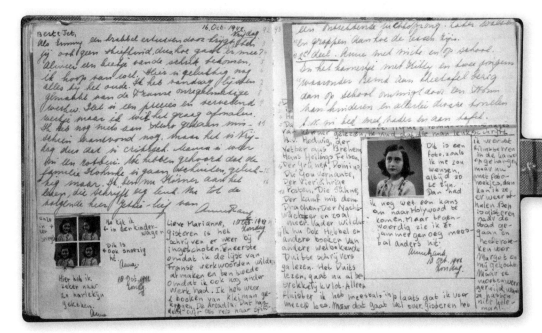

One of the world's most famous diaries

DIARIES

At this early-21st-century moment, diary-keeping seems to be a major industry. It's easy to find not only actual diaries—usually leather-bound, gilt-edged, and posh, with dates and a fixed amount of space for each day—but also blank bound books that accommodate themselves to both natterers and minimalists. These come in all price ranges and styles, from the exotic (Tibetan Fair Trade Himalayan Lokta paper books handcrafted in Nepal) to the classic (Moleskines, "the legendary notebook used by European artists and thinkers for the past two centuries," including Van Gogh and Hemingway), from the humdrum (the inexplicably popular "Anything Books" with their football-textured covers) to the gross (flimsy spiral ones with distorted, cartoony dog pictures on them at my local Stop & Shop).

Keeping a diary is often referred to as "journaling," and there are dozens of books and websites giving instructions for how to do it, and why, and with what.[8] The activity is

8 This despite the critic Louis Menand's probably true observation: "The impulse to keep a diary is to actual diaries as the impulse to go on a diet is to actual slimness."

recommended for grieving, for "healing," for recovering, for spiritual questing, for posterity, for "stress management," for fun, for discipline, for publication. (One poignant title on the subject is Alexandra Johnson's *Leaving a Trace*, which perhaps says it all.) There are tips for journaling with the Tarot or with the Bible, for overcoming "journaler's block," for digging into your dreams, for tapping your inner wisdom and getting it down on paper while it's hot, for combining journaling with "scrapbooking."

The journaling advisers are sympathetic and understanding about bad penmanship. If your script is hard to read— widely discussed as a common problem—they advise typing your journal, maybe combining computer-generated text with some handwritten bits. One journaling coach humorously advises, "Include some of your own handwriting so your descendants will know why you decided to type," but points out that, when we come across an old diary in the attic, we're not usually overly concerned about whether Great-aunt Gertrude's penmanship was any good—though it would be frustrating if it were completely illegible.[9]

Aside from some avid computer journalers and a huge fad for not only blogs but intimate and personal online diaries—a growth industry for exhibitionists[10]—most diaries are written as they've always been, by hand. And rightly so. Writing in a little book, with an implement, invites contemplation, the kind of slow, far-ranging, digressive thinking that can clarify knotty problems or come up with a telling adjective. Some advocates of old-fashioned diary-keeping even believe that writing in a beautiful book inspires not only beautiful thoughts but beautiful script. (This can backfire: someone once brought me back from Venice a gorgeous hand-marbled notebook tied with a silky ribbon, and it took me about eight years to summon the nerve to use it.) Others feel that writing by hand is important as a reflection of your mood: the diary is

9 It wouldn't be: everyone named Gertrude was thoroughly instructed in penmanship in school.

10 Last time I checked, there were more than 7000 of them listed on the diarist. net site. One diarist confesses that she loves the Victorian Age, believes in ghosts, and has a drinking problem. Another hates her underwear and likes taking pictures of penguins.

the place for angry scribbles, dramatic underlining, forests of exclamation points. And now and then one might like to insert a drawing—impossible with a computer unless you draw it on paper and scan it in, which seems guaranteed to destroy the mood, whatever it was.

One of the obvious advantages of the pen-and-notebook routine is its portability. I finally used the Venetian notebook, appropriately, as a travel journal when I was in Italy myself. Reading it now, I see the tiny red lizards that lived under the steps, smell the rosemary that grew three feet high along the stone path, hear the tourists next door arguing stridently in German about where to have dinner....

In a 2008 essay in the *Chronicle of Higher Education*, the writer and professor Mark Edmundson writes about a friend who calls his forty-year-long diary a "life thickener." Edmundson comments, "His quotations and pictures and clips and drawings and paintings give density and meaning to the blind onrush that life can be." In a similar spirit, I have kept a diary for most of my life—a tendency I may have inherited from my mother. Mom strenuously denied that she kept a diary, which she seemed to consider a silly bit of self-indulgence. She always said, "I just jot things down." She made her jottings on the grids of a wall calendar, quickly and informally. I have a stack of her old calendars—usually free-bies given away by the bank— and she never wrote anything more personal than "Very bad cold! Stayed home from Mass!" or a notation every January 20 of exactly how many years my father had been dead. Her calendars from my babyhood record immunizations and solid food ("baby loves carrots!") and the occasional adorable saying.

I have a long shelf of published diaries—mostly those of writers, and therefore pretty well written, but I'm not fussy. I've seldom met a diary I didn't like, and fame and a good prose style are not requirements. Years ago, a friend found a leather

five-year "Line-a-Day" diary in a junk shop and, knowing I'm
a diary nut, turned it over to me.

The Latin inscription on the first page is "Nulla dies sine
linea" ("No day without a line"), and it was indeed kept faith-
fully in flawless Palmer Method by a woman named Florence,
who lived in Warren, Massachusetts. She had brown hair and
light blue eyes, she was five feet four inches tall, and she had
narrow little feet (her shoe size was 6½ AAA). She baked rolls
on a regular basis, canned vegetables from her garden, made
soap, played bridge, and sang in the choir. Her diary begins
on January 1, 1940, with a chicken pie and a visit from Miss
French, and ends on December 31, 1944, with rain and slush on
"a very quiet day." She writes about nothing very much, and
her entries fascinate me.

There's an intriguing compromise available for someone who has terrific handwriting but is too lazy/tired/stressed/arthritic/technology-crazed to write by hand, an outfit called Fontifier (www.fontifier.com), which will—surprisingly cheaply—turn your script into a font you can install into your computer. Fontifier urges us to use their product to add a "personal touch" to journals, cards, letters, etc.—the only trouble being, of course, that the font will lack the variations of normal handwriting. In other words, it won't fool anyone. But it's an undeniably cool idea, particularly their off-the-wall suggestion that you can use it for "secret writing systems," something that would have enormous appeal for the average twelve-year-old.

SYMPATHY NOTES, THANK-YOU NOTES, AND WEDDING INVITATIONS

Handwritten letters are as rare as a purple three-cent Thomas Jefferson stamp from 1957. At this point, the only handwritten ones I receive are from a former aunt-in-law who's well into her eighties. I suspect that there are some poor souls in this world who have never had their mailboxes graced with such a thing.

I actually love email, which enables me to keep on top of a large correspondence easily and quickly. But the drab click of a key as you slump in front of the computer is a far cry from the happy slash of a letter opener as you sprawl on the sofa with your feet up. TV didn't kill off radio, air-conditioning didn't destroy electric fans, cars didn't displace bicycles. But cheap long-distance rates and the ubiquity of email have sent letter-writing to the land of the dodo.

And yet a long, chatty, funny letter full of private jokes and sly allusions and witty asides and low gossip is the pinnacle of postal bliss. No matter what its subject, a letter speaks in the writer's voice, and it does it better than a phone call: you can't sit down and reread a phone call.[11]

11 To which Lord Byron might add, "One of the pleasures of re-reading old letters is the knowledge that they need no answer." But that was a joke: Byron was one of the world's great correspondents, and his collected letters fill many volumes.

However, although the "friendly letter" (as they called it in school back in the days when you'd be learning to write one in your best Palmer Method) is well on its way to biting the dust, the tradition of hand-writing certain specialized kinds of communications lingers, as a last desperate grasp at individuality and personal expression, a visible sign of *caring* in the midst of the vast impersonality that surrounds us.

According to every etiquette book I've consulted, sympathy notes should always be written by hand. There are times when nothing can replace the sincerity of pen on paper, no matter how ugly the script or bad the punctuation. Those somber, white, be-lilied and be-prayered sympathy cards from the drugstore just don't cut it: there's no substitute, says the etiquette guru Amy Vanderbilt, for your own thoughts and feelings[12] expressed on your personal stationery (meaning plain, white, and printed with your name) in black or blue-black ink *only*—and no smudgy ballpoints! If your handwriting tends to be sloppy—well, just try harder.

Thank-you notes provide more leeway, though the official policy of the etiquette books is that if you send out a commercial thank-you card you're a total clod. This is especially important for brides (grooms are apparently allowed to go out and play golf). Printed thank-you notes seem acceptable to me—jeez, people are busy—but Miss Manners says she's "fussier than ever about letters of thanks being handwritten," and even *Etiquette for Dummies* is surprisingly old-fashioned, coming down hard on the side of handwritten thank-you notes, "on good quality stationery," with no smudges or crossings out, and preferably with a fountain pen—warning that you should never let anyone borrow yours because the nib wears down in an individual way and someone else's handwriting will screw it up. (My Belgian friend Danièle tells me that, when she was around twelve and tried to borrow her father's fountain pen, he handed her a biro and said, "There are three things a man never lends out: his car, his wife, or his fountain pen.")

12 As Leon Edel pointed out in his biography of Henry James, "His condolences were so fine, so properly measured and elegantly turned, they seemed almost worth dying for."

Then there are hand-addressed wedding invitations. It's always a shock—a rather happy one—to find, amidst the junk mail and the bills, one of those thick, creamy envelopes with its elegant script. Except for the outrageous price of the stamp, all of a sudden we're back in 1953, or 1878. Awesomely beautiful handwriting! Right there in your mailbox!

Dr. & Mrs. Andrew Mackenzie

13850 NW Forest Park Drive

Manzanita · Maine · 97264

Now there are "calligraphy style" computer fonts that approximate hand-lettering and are used by most commercial "invitation vendors." But a surprising number of brides continue to employ a calligrapher, even if it's only a friend with a broad-nib pen.

CALLIGRAPHY

True calligraphy (from the Greek for "beautiful writing") becomes more endangered with every technological incursion into its traditional territory. But, like literary fiction and heirloom tomatoes, calligraphy survives as a niche market, supported by a small but fiercely enthusiastic band of practitioners and supporters.

On a trip to New York City, I went to a show of the work of Saul Steinberg at the Morgan Library. Everyone loves Steinberg: his whimsical *New Yorker* covers, his wacky cats, the cartoon skyscrapers and strange geometries and witty maps. What I like most, though, is what he does with words, letters, numbers, music—and handwriting. I have hanging on my study wall a magnificent Steinberg poster—one of his celebrated phony documents, executed in elaborate script, stuck with official-looking stamps and seals, and signifying exactly nothing.

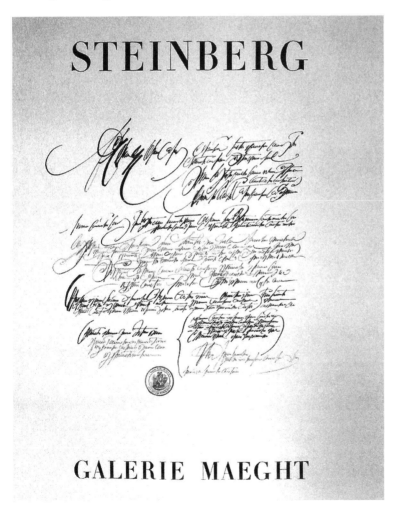

Steinberg (1914–1999), a Rumanian Jew living in Italy under the Fascist regime, escaped in 1941 thanks to a passport he doctored himself with a flurry of "official" red stamps; it enabled him to make his way, via Lisbon, to America. Since then, a stream of his dazzlingly unreadable calligraphy has adorned fake certificates, passports, and diplomas; it sprouts from the heads of humans and the mouths of dogs; it covers a pair of convincingly coffee-spotted and messy diary pages (which Steinberg playfully claimed were Rimbaud's). "Calligraphy," he once said, "is my true teacher."

The Steinberg selections at the Morgan were, in fact, full of handwriting. And, though Steinberg had no such intent—and died before the digital age was in full swing—the fact that most of it is meaningless and unreadable seems an emblem of the sorry situation handwriting is in today, when it's seen as a useless archaic skill, a fading flower kept precariously in bloom.

Among those tending it are the "real" calligraphers, the folks who bring you those hand-written envelopes. They also design logos, letter diplomas, produce menus for restaurants, and occasionally get some work creating film titles. The

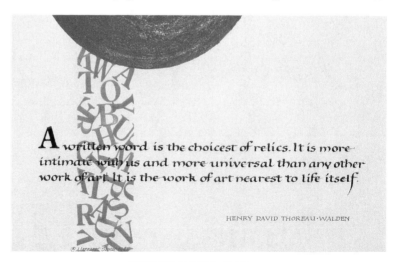

A written word is the choicest of relics. It is more intimate with us and more universal than any other work of art. It is the work of art nearest to life itself.

HENRY DAVID THOREAU·WALDEN

Calligraphy by Margaret Soucy

Queen of England has her own official scribe. The White House supports a hefty staff of calligraphers busy with invitations, place cards, award certificates, and various official documents. Greeting card companies employ crews of letterers and use hundreds of freelancers. And many calligraphers have moved beyond calligraphy into the realm of fine art, as in the work of Connecticut calligrapher Margaret Soucy, who prefers the term "lettering artist."

The English artist and calligrapher Sheila Waters studied for her Master's degree at London's Royal College of Art with Dorothy Mahoney, who was an assistant to the great lettering pioneer Edward Johnston. Johnston's famous work *Writing and Illuminating and Lettering*, the "calligrapher's bible," has been called "the best handbook ever written on any subject" by Sir Sidney Cockerell, curator of the Fitzwilliam Museum at Cambridge—himself a prolific diarist and handwriting buff.

Waters was only twenty-two when, in 1951, she was elected a Fellow of the Society of Scribes and Illuminators—meaning that, even at that youthful stage in her career, she was recognized by her peers to be "at the pinnacle of achievement." She went on to an illustrious career doing commissions for royalty, museums, libraries, collectors, and publishers. Her book *Foundations of Calligraphy* has earned its own place as a classic text.

When she moved to America in the 1970s Waters co-founded the Washington (D.C.) Calligraphers Guild and helped fuel what became a calligraphy mini-revival in this country. The '70s represented the fading twilight of the pre-computer era, the last gasp of letter-writing, a time when it was far from unusual to open your mailbox and see the handwriting of a friend on an envelope. Calligraphy became briefly hot. Everyone was investing in a broad-nib pen. For a while we all improved our handwriting, producing a script that looked kind of like calligraphy, but was essentially our regular scrawl enhanced by shading. Most of us, needless to say, didn't become profession-als, and eventually our pens and ink bottles were left behind somewhere along with the bell-bottoms and love beads.

But some people never looked back. As calligraphy courses proliferated, those who remained under the spell of letters per-severed, studied, practiced, formed guilds, held conferences, founded newsletters, and sometimes began to make a living.

The appeal of beautiful calligraphy comes, in part, from the astounding variety that can be spawned by a fixed collec-tion of twenty-six letters and ten number forms, combining day-to-day familiarity with boundless possibilities—the meeting of the mundane and the magnificent.

Calligraphy can be purely traditional, adhering strictly to some historical script or working subtle changes on it. Sheila Waters's monumental illuminated calligraphic man-uscript of Dylan Thomas's *Under Milk Wood* was done in a variation on ninth-century Carolingian Minuscule. As she explained in an interview, "I sharpened the club-shaped ascender serifs, omitted archaic parts, and accentuated the 'bounce' of the italic-like branching in *n* and *m* by slanting the writing about four degrees."

she grew in the dark until long-dead
Gomer Owen kissed her when she wasn't
looking because he was dared. Now in
the light she'll work, sing, milk, say the
cows' sweet names and sleep until the
night sucks out her soul and spits it into
the sky. In her life-long love light, holily
Bessie milks the fond lake-eyed cows as
dusk showers slowly down over byre, sea
and town.

From Under Milk Wood *by Dylan Thomas*

Or it can be an exuberantly original offspring of the calligrapher's own sensibility. The astounding website www.omniglot.com, which is a guide to world writing systems, also includes a section of personal alphabets, among them the runelike "Runtrikha":

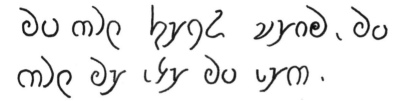

Translation: The more things change,
the more they stay the same.

and "Vine," a vertically arranged system that looks like intricate dangling earrings:

Translation: Can a man walk on hot coals and
his feet not be scorched?

Byron's graffito at the Temple of Poseidon, in Attica

GRAFFITI

As an ex–New Yorker, I know what it is to live with graffiti painted on every bare wall, every phone booth, every advertising sign—on sidewalks, water towers, the sides of buses, the doorways of venerable brownstones. In the rapidly gentrifying Brooklyn neighborhood I used to live in, it was often in Polish, and the most popular graffito was some variant of YUPPIE GO HOME.

The urgent need to write things for public view in a prominent place has been with us since people learned to write. It appears in all cultures. The Greeks and Romans did it. The Vikings did it. The Chinese did it on the Great Wall. Michelangelo did it in the ruins of Nero's villa. That mad, bad, and dangerous-to-know Byron did it in Greece, in 1810, quite prettily.

When I visited Glastonbury Abbey in England I was stunned by the dense hodgepodge of eighteenth-and-nineteenth-century graffiti carved into its soft stone walls. Hoboes in 1930s America scrawled their names on the freight cars they hopped. The ubiquitous KILROY WAS HERE was here, there, and everywhere in the '40s, perpetrated by G.I.'s in Europe—no one knows why:

KILROY WAS
HERE

People routinely sign home-made cement walks with their initials and the date. My friend Eileen stood on a chair and penciled her signature discreetly on the wallpaper above every doorframe in her family's apartment. Antiwar slogans were rife during the '60s. Simple gang markers began to be seen in the '70s. And then there were the heart-rending post-9/11 memorials in New York City.

Today, when most Americans think of graffiti, we don't think of tastefully carved Roman capitals or quaint obscenities like FUTUI COPONAM[13] or a simple name or political message. We think of the miles and miles of spray-painted tagging that defaces buildings in big cities. Much of it is downright ugly, and most people instinctively recoil from it: it's incomprehensible, it's intrusive, it's pointless, and until you get used to it, it seems threatening. But it's impossible to ignore—and that, of course, is why it's there.

In 1971, the *New York Times* validated graffiti as a cultural phenomenon in an article about a writer whose tag, TAKI 183, was plastered all over the city. (Taki was an otherwise mainstream, well-behaved kid named Demitrius who lived on 183rd Street. His modest explanation for his compulsion to wield his black magic marker all over the city was a shrugged "You do it for yourself.") Many graffiti historians claim that, from that moment, graffiti as we know it began to spread not only around New York, but around the world. Others say that it began in Philadelphia a year earlier. Wherever it was born, it proliferated like a kind of urban kudzu.

It was also rapidly evolving. Markers were replaced by spray paint. Simple name tags morphed into big, fat-lettered signatures in wild color schemes. Writing on trash cans and doorways gave way to elaborate decorations on the mega-canvases known as subway trains.[14] Legible bubble letters and 3-D alphabets gave way to what was known as the often unreadable, abstract "Wildstyle" that was carefully planned out in advance and usually executed by crews of artists.[15] The bigger, the bolder, the more visible, the better, because graffiti was no longer done for "yourself," it was about being seen by the world, competing with your peers, getting recognition, making your mark—literally.

13 "I screwed the barmaid," preserved in the ruins of Pompeii.

14 The MTA turned to a combination of razor-wire, guard dogs, graffiti-proof paint, and regular scrubbing, and finally, by 1988, had pretty much wiped it out. Diehards still scratch with a sharp object on the cars' walls and windows, but the results are, to say the least, lame.

15 In other words, graffiti evolution began to parallel the history of handwriting through the ages: simple to complex to supremely difficult to write and read.

Modern graffiti artists have little in common with young Byron scratching his name on a wall in Greece, and the value of what they produce is the subject of impassioned debate. Graffiti is vandalism perpetrated by antisocial punks—or it's a colorful, vibrantly creative art form that deserves to be recognized as such. The two points of view are alive and well. Graffiti writers are both prosecuted in court (2,962 arrests in New York City in 2006) and enshrined in art exhibits.

Some graffiti—lots of it, actually—is hideous, offensive, a mess. But the bold originality of graffiti alphabets is undeniable.

And even as I'm thinking one of the best things about graffiti is that there's no way a computer could do this kind of thing, I'm chagrined to discover that there are dozens of graffiti fonts available.

HANDWRITING ORGANIZATIONS

The concept of "slow writing" humorously suggested in the *Oregonian* is not an idle dream. It's actually a burgeoning movement produced, and promoted, by organizations like IAMPETH, the International Association of Master Penmen, Engrossers[16] and Teachers of Handwriting. To say this organization is a throwback to another time would be unfair in view of its 400-strong membership, its quarterly newsletter (*Penman's Journal*), its vast and fascinating website, its

16 An engrosser, using an elaborate, formal, slowly executed roundhand, inscribes information onto official documents, like legal resolutions.

lively Ornamental Penman Discussion Group on Yahoo, and its annual convention, which in 2008 was on the West Coast so that fervent members of the Japan Penmanship Association (not to mention those from western Canada and Mexico) could more conveniently take part.

One thing that I've learned after many years of poking into oddball corners of culture for purposes of research or out of simple nosiness is that the world is indeed full of a number of things.[17] Who knew there was a National Pie Day?[18] Or that cotton candy at the circus in Madison Square Garden is going to set you back twelve bucks? Or that Mohammed's pet cat, Muezza, was once sleeping on his cloak and, rather than disturb her, Mohammed cut around the cat with scissors and wore the cloak with a hole in it? Or that gray whales love to have their bellies scratched, the average American walks a mile and a half a week, and Edith Wharton secretly loathed her friend Henry James's later novels?

And who knew that there are active associations of enthusiasts dedicated to practicing and preserving the fabulously fancy, flourished hands of the eighteenth and nineteenth centuries? That copperplate is still avidly practiced? That Spencerian is galloping along, alive and well? As a former president of IAMPETH, Rick Muffler, put it, "There's a theory that computers are going to replace us, but it's not going to happen. They make what we do even more valuable."

IAMPETH is the oldest and largest penmanship association in the United States, and the goal of its membership is to "preserve and share with others the rich tradition of American Penmanship." The organization confers a Master Penman certificate: each master writes his or her own. (Penman as used here is a unisex term.)

The calligraphy world is pleasantly stocked with organizations whose purpose is to promote the art, hold classes and workshops, sponsor exhibits, introduce calligraphy into the schools, and—quite often—produce a newsletter full of calli-

17 From Robert Louis Stevenson's *A Child's Garden of Verses*: "The world is so full of a number of things/ I'm sure we should all be as happy as kings," to which James Thurber appended sarcastically, "And you know how happy kings are."

18 January 23, same as National Handwriting Day: maybe a good day to make a pie and then write out the recipe in neat, legible script and pass it on to a friend?

graphic art and articles on such matters as monogram design, making your own paper, and the joy of Roman Half-Uncial. The Association for the Calligraphic Arts is an umbrella organization, and most states have at least one individual guild. Oregon has seven.

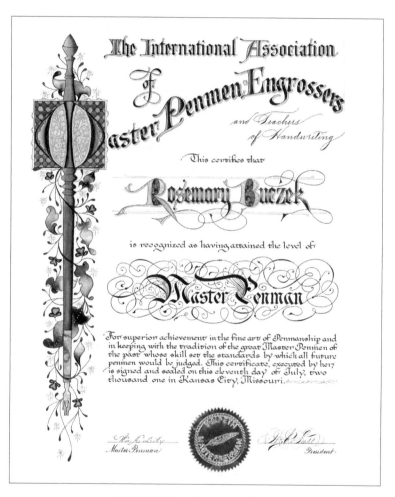

IAMPETH Master Penman certificate

One of my favorite passionate penmanship promotion programs is run by Michael Sull (a past president of IAMPETH).
Sull learned ornamental penmanship from one of the art's
old masters: Paul O'Hara, who boasted, "I'm ninety years old
but I can still throw a pen." Sull put in his time at Hallmark
Cards, which eventually decided his preferred script was "too
ornate" and booted him off the staff. He says it's the best thing
that ever happened to him. In 1986 ("I couldn't let it die") he
began teaching Spencerian penmanship in Kansas. He and his
wife, Deb, are now full-time Spencerian penmen. They conduct workshops all over the country, as well as in Europe and
Japan (where, perhaps because of its long calligraphic tradition, Spencerian has as many fans as it does in the U.S.).[19]
Sull has also devised a handwriting curriculum for schools,
using a script he has aptly dubbed American Cursive, a syn-
thesis of the work of Palmer and the other great American
penmen. He has boiled it all down to what, for him, are the
most important fundamentals—and, for Sull, "most important" encompasses "most beautiful," an idea Spencer himself
would have surely approved of. Sull's true love is Spencerian
script—though he writes and teaches a more highly ornate
version than the "everyday" Spencerian of the workbooks—
and his hope is that the American Cursive program will be a
kind of gateway drug, gently nudging students along a road
on which the next stop is vintage Spencerian cursive and the
final destination is true ornamental penmanship, with its
thicks and thins, its flourishes and frills, and its prominent
position in America's rich cultural history.

What most intrigued me about Sull's work is the annual
weeklong Spencerian Saga Workshops (traditional and
advanced), held every autumn in Geneva-on-the-Lake, Ohio,
since 1986.

19 The Japan Penmanship
Association's
newsletter, Yoshodo,
has been published
since 1946.

The Spenciarian Saga Workshop logo

"Join us for a visit back in time to America's Golden Age of Penmanship," the website exhorts. The menu includes a hefty entrée of Spencerian script, with side dishes of Off-Hand Flourishing, Monogram Design, and a study of "The Secret of the Skill of Madarasz."[20] Best of all, for what I, at least, would consider dessert, participants take a field trip to the Evergreen Cemetery in nearby Ashtabula, where they make rubbings of Platt Rogers Spencer's memorial with its stupendous three-foot quill pen.

Sull is eloquent on the subject of good handwriting. "Penmanship these days is thought of as a vestigial organ because it's not translated into dollars, like computer skills," he says. "But if you need to relay information immediately and have just a half-second to grab anything, maybe just a napkin, penmanship is so valuable. It doesn't rely on batteries or power. It's like breathing—it's always with you."

Today Spencerian is something of a fine art, but for half a century it was the basic everyday script of educated Americans. I was curious to see what it would be like to go back in time and give it a try. I took my oblique pen in hand and, after a demanding but enjoyable ink-stained hour with Michael Sull's very well-made instructional video, this is what I produced (left).

20 Which sounds like some occult practice or the eighth Harry Potter, but is a book about the work of the celebrated Louis Madarasz (1859–1910), often called the most highly skilled ornamental penman who ever lived.

Author's Spencerian script

PEN COLLECTORS

Writing with a good fountain pen is supremely pleasurable in a way that's hard to describe. It involves both the necessity of writing a bit more slowly (which instantly improves my own deteriorated day-to-day script), and the way the letters look as they form at the base of the graceful tapered triangle. This experience inspires a surprising amount of lyrical reflection among pen people—and there are still plenty of pen people in this world. I'm one of them.

All through high school, even after the transition to ballpoints, I remained nostalgically, almost romantically attached to my Esterbrook fountain pen.

The Esterbrooks had barrels of marbled celluloid, they came in tastefully muted colors, and, best of all, they had interchangeable screw-in pen points, so that you could vary your handwriting—make it thinner, thicker, more shaded—simply by changing the nib.

In college, I clung to my fountain pen. It was better suited than a ballpoint to the affected and precious quasi-printing I cultivated, especially in the self-consciously literary letters I wrote to friends—though I sometimes typed them, too, usually sitting on my bed with my portable typewriter on my lap.

*Esterbrook
"Dollar Pen"*

*My roommate, Sara, with
her "laptop," 1963*

Parker 75

The Pennant *magazine*

21 In addition, there are the
equally pen-crazed
magazines Pen World
International and Stylus.

When I graduated from college, my then-boyfriend gave me a Parker 75, a very classy and expensive pen with an arrow-shaped 14-carat gold clip and an interesting grid pattern.

I worshiped that pen. It seemed to me the zenith of sophistication—the pen of a real writer. I used it constantly for a few years, then brought it out only for special occasions, then chucked it into the drawer where one chucks things one doesn't use but can't bear to throw out. At some point it disappeared, as things do. I wish I still had it.

As with almost anything you can think of, fountain pens have their own fan base and are highly collectible. Every year, at least half a dozen major pen shows are held across the country, and there's an Esterbrook chat room on Yahoo. Pen Collectors of America is another of those wonderfully peculiar organizations full of people who are ardently keen on a tiny piece of American culture—in this case, the fountain pen. It began in Southern California in the 1980s, when a group of pen enthusiasts who used to run into each other at flea markets decided to get together at someone's house and talk pens. In the miraculous way that these things happen, their fame spread, their membership grew, and today there are nearly two thousand of them. The primary mission of their organization is to "foster and maintain the integrity of pen collecting" and "promote the use of fountain pens." They publish *The Pennant*, which features articles with intriguing titles like "A Penman's Walk Through Downtown L.A.," "Collecting Japanese Pens," and "Smoothing Scratchy Nibs," as well as book reviews, lists of pen shows and repair shops, and impassioned letters to the editor.[21]

Making a wooden fountain pen from scratch is probably the most extreme Nostalgia Planet pastime, and yet there are quite a few books and articles devoted to the subject. It does have a certain nutty charm. You're going to need your lathe, your mandrel and bushings, your locking nut, your collet, your pen tube insertion tool and glue, possibly a hex wrench and a squaring jig, and, of course, the wood: Bolivian Rosewood, Bubinga, Zebrawood, Granadillo, Cocobolo, Yellowheart, Ebony, Curly Maple.... Just reciting their names makes the true pen nut dream about rolling up her sleeves and getting to work.

* * * *

I took a stroll through the pen department at a nearby office-supply store, fifty feet of writing implements: ballpoints, fountain pens, rollerballs, gel pens, felt-tips, highlighters, bold points, fine points, superfine points, micro points, needle points, comfort grips, super-comfy grips, rubber grips, precision grips, non-slip grips, classic grips, water-resistant pens, fade-resistant pens, airplane-safe pens ("won't leak in flight"), pens "specially formulated to help prevent check fraud," latex-free pens, "go-anywhere" pens ("clip it, hang it, wear it"), erasable pens, expandable pens, pens with built-in highlighters, "won't bleed thru paper" pens, permanent markers, washable markers, china markers, click pencils, pencils that support breast cancer research, refillable pencils, never-need-sharpening pencils, drafting pencils, antimicrobial pencils....

I was dazzled. I buy way too many of these doodads.

The cornucopia in the pen aisle represents mega-marketing and mass production at their most extreme. It can't be only pen crazies and nostalgia buffs, dazed by inky abundance, who are buying this stuff. We all write. Some of us like it, some hate it. Some write well, others badly. A lot of us try to write more legibly, vow to improve. But scrawling things with pens and pencils on pieces of paper is something we all do. There's no getting around it. As one of my calligrapher friends put it: "Try to go through the day without writing anything down."

Author's desk

Chapter Five

Is Handwriting Important?

Students are usually taught to print in first grade, which is when my own generation learned it. In those long-gone days, the move from printing to cursive writing in third grade was a ritual of growing up, an entry into the adult world.

But today, for many students, handwriting instruction doesn't go beyond that—and some people believe it shouldn't. Just as, back in the eighteenth century, cacography (poor penmanship) was considered a mark of the leisured class, there are plenty of people today who accept their own atrocious writing without a qualm, who don't intend to write badly but see no practical use for a legibility they were never taught. An editor I know comments, "I'd rather see people learn grammar and usage and spelling than neat handwriting. You can write a beautiful script and still look like an idiot if you mix up *imply* and *infer*." True enough! As a copy editor, I wish *They had to flea their village* and *He was a child protégé on the violin* hadn't just come across my desk.

Other proud cacographers believe bad writing is a way of declaring their individuality and creativity, their refusal to truckle under and write like a nun or a schoolteacher. Tamara Plakins Thornton, in *Handwriting in America*, comes out strongly as a pro-printing, pro-keyboarding, anti-cursive, pro-technology anti-Luddite. For her, penmanship study can be an exercise in conformity. All her life, Thornton has had a "secret conviction that good penmanship does not matter, that if anything it denotes a person who is fearful or incapable of being in any way unusual." To me, in our computerized world, it's beautiful handwriting that seems unusual, a mark of individuality. A low-tech friend of mine with a thriving garden design business in Manhattan sends out handwritten bills on her elegant stationery. Her customers love it.

Among the advocates of reviving penmanship exercises, some may really be looking for a return of the discipline that was forced on children in their own day. This is the dark underbelly of nostalgia, something that we who were raised in a simpler, more picturesque time (sock hops and taffy pulls, sledding down Maple Street Hill, tying on a gingham apron and helping Mom bake bread) need to be on guard against. I would love to see children writing cursive script, just because it seems wrong when something beautiful, useful, and historically important vanishes. But underneath the Norman Rockwell stuff, many of us were severely over-disciplined children, and so the idea can also be rather discomfiting. We don't need to inflict our suffering on a new generation of innocent babes. My own daughter never finickily ironed the wrinkles out of a handkerchief in her life, much less sprinkled one with water and let it sit until it was "ready," and yet as an adult she seems to be a pretty solid citizen.

However, there are better arguments for learning to write neatly than "Those were the good old days." There's an increasing body of evidence that says good handwriting can influence academic performance on many levels. Dennis Williams, the national product manager for the Zaner-Bloser school handwriting program—one of the most popular in use today—

points out that handwriting is not an isolated skill. For young students, the primary goal is to learn to read fluently—as Williams puts it, "to crack the code of the alphabet"—and, as they write their letters, they're matching symbols to sounds. They not only see the letters and hear the way they sound, they actually create them, on paper, with care. In addition, they are able to get a clear idea of which letters are commonly associated with each other—a necessity for good spelling.

I also talked to Louise Spear-Swerling, a learning disabilities specialist who teaches at Southern Connecticut State University in New Haven. She is firmly committed to the idea that handwriting instruction is especially beneficial not merely to learning-disabled kids but to all children at the early stage when they're trying to master letter sounds. "Writing focuses their attention," she says. "Just looking at a letter isn't going to do it." Spear-Swerling has respect for the usefulness of computers and word-processing programs for children with writing problems, but, along with every educator I spoke to, she strongly believes that advances in technology do not eliminate the need for teaching handwriting.

When young children learn handwriting at the same time that they're learning to express their thoughts on paper, the two kinds of writing—one a mechanical skill, one a creative intellectual process—become naturally and inextricably connected in the child's mind. In a 2006 article in *Developmental Neuropsychology*, Steven T. Peverly of Columbia University Teachers College elaborates on this idea: "For both children and adults, research suggests that greater transcription speed increases automaticity of word production" so that a writer's working memory can be freed up "for the metacognitive processes needed to create good reader-friendly prose."

In other words, students need to write not only clearly but also quickly—the less we have to struggle with making a capital *G*, the more we can think about what we're trying to say and how to say it.

While it's true that learning a legible handwriting is not easy for young children—gratification isn't immediate but slow and cumulative—there may be an intrinsic and lasting value in having children deal with this kind of frustration. The classic "marshmallow test" done in the 1960s by the Stanford psychologist Walter Mischel (now at Columbia) illustrates this: a plate of marshmallows was put in front of a group of four-year-olds. The children were told they could take a marshmallow—or, if they waited fifteen minutes, they could have two marshmallows. Some of them—the hedonistic set—grabbed one immediately and wolfed it down. Others chose to wait, even though delaying gratification was so painful that some had to close their eyes so they couldn't see the marshmallows. Fourteen years later, the kids were evaluated. Sure enough, the ones who'd been able to wait had more friends, better social skills, and higher grades and SAT scores than the grabbers, who were often in academic trouble. Mischel's study doesn't comment, but chances are the waiters had better handwriting as well.

In school, a student's slovenly script, regardless of its content, almost always carries a penalty: the cacography-plagued Duke of Wellington wouldn't have made it out of sixth grade:

For one thing, if the writing is indecipherable chicken-scratching, what's written, brilliant or not, is beside the point—no one can read it. For another, bad handwriting implies that the writer doesn't care about the reader. By the time a teacher has strained to make out whether it's *book* or *look* or *boob* or *Bob* or *kook* or *boat* or *lob* or *load*....Well, that teacher has become alienated. D-minus.

But young children want to learn to write; they see it as a natural, desirable, inevitable process. They begin drawing as soon as their small-motor skills permit them to hold a pencil or a paintbrush, and they instinctively scribble letter-like forms: they see their elders writing and want to imitate them.

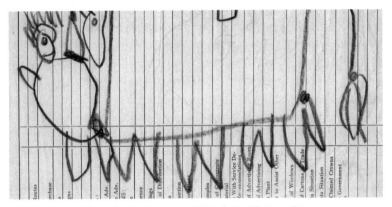

The author's obsession with the letter W *at age three*

As Charles L. Lehman puts it in *Handwriting Models for Schools*: "From about the age of three, slanting verticals and elliptical scribbles appear with more consistency." If they're read to by adults, kids are quick to grasp the connection between spoken words and words on a page, and to understand how letters "work"—left to right, in straight lines, with strategic spaces. By the time they're five or six years old, they're ready to write, both physically and psychologically.

The trick for a teacher is to nurture that instinct, not squelch it. Learning to write well is challenging, but it doesn't have to be a daunting task. Most contemporary handwriting programs stress the idea that kids will not dread or dislike it if the teacher stays positive, reinforces what they do well—and doesn't let the lesson go on too long. In the 1950s, the average time spent practicing Palmer Method approached two hours a week. Now the average is more like fifteen minutes a day, maybe three times a week, and that seems to be enough. Most handwriting programs, including Zaner-Bloser, have gradually become shorter, snappier, adapted to brief attention spans and diminished class time.

What's vitally important, however, is following up this early instruction. When I was in school, handwriting practice continued through the fifth grade—and no one was allowed to get away with illegible script, right up to graduation day. Now, if handwriting is taught at all, it ends just as the demands of school are requiring children to write more often, and more rapidly. Kathy Libby, a former teacher and the author of a series of handwriting workbooks, says that if students haven't mastered cursive by the end of third grade, it's over. Cursive is only "randomly reinforced" after that. Teachers may reprimand students for bad handwriting, or plead with them to write more neatly, or take off points for sloppiness, but that's it. "Not many fourth-grade teachers currently teach cursive, leaving non-fluent third graders at risk," Libby says. "These students are at a disadvantage." Without reinforcement, a student's script can gradually deteriorate into the illegibility that afflicts so many adults.

And like it or not, even in our machine-driven world, people still judge you by your handwriting. In businesses that continue to require handwritten applications, it's a truism that job candidates with a pleasing script tend to be hired over those who scribble. I recently experienced this first hand: judging handwritten applications for writing positions, I found myself drawn to those with legible handwriting and prejudiced against the scrawlers; in every case, the better handwriters turned out to be better writers as well.

A surprising number of help-wanted ads require applicants to have not only proficiency in MS Word, and Excel, but also "neat handwriting." Or maybe this isn't really so surprising: according to the Writing Instrument Manufacturers Association, cacography-caused business losses—phone calls made to wrong numbers, incorrect items shipped, sloppy tax returns, undeliverable letters and packages, secretaries unable to read their bosses' handwriting—hover around $200 million annually.

* * * *

But, as many struggling handwriters have probably asked themselves: Do we really need to learn cursive writing? How is it superior to printing?

I may have been brainwashed at an impressionable age by Sister Victorine and the Palmer Method, but I always assumed that cursive writing was rapid writing—that it's not called "cursive" (which means, roughly, "running") for nothing. I began to doubt this when my daughter, Katherine, told me that the reason her handwriting has evolved from the cursive drilled into her in third grade to a highly individual printed style with a few cursive touches is that:

This is quicker!

The standard argument against printing by fans of traditional cursive is that the writer has to keep lifting the pen from the paper, and this wastes time. This is simply not true: lifting the pen once in a while and moving it through the air a quarter of an inch takes no more time than dragging it a quarter of an inch across the paper. And it saves ink. And it gives the hand a nanosecond of rest. In an admittedly unscientific test, I was surprised at how much less stressed my writing hand felt when it had the little breaks you get with the print/cursive combo.

I asked Steve Graham, a professor of special education at Vanderbilt University who has written extensively on how handwriting develops, if printing is more legible, but cursive is quicker. It depends, he says. Cursive may indeed be faster for people who have been using it all their lives. It's their natural script, learned long ago, and it tends to be an efficient one for them. In a study focused on ways to improve writing skills, Graham and his colleagues, looking at students in grades one through six, found that cursive and printing had the same degree of readability—but that the speediest writers were those who mixed the two, using a combination of printing and cursive that joins only certain selected letters, usually the easiest ones to link up.

In 2006, a mere 15 percent of the students taking the SATs wrote their essays in cursive; everyone else printed. The cursive essays had, on average, only slightly higher scores than printed ones, according to the College Board—not enough to be statistically valid.[1] Neat and legible printing, or half-printing—whether good to look at or merely serviceable—is definitely preferable to dutiful, earnest, sloppy cursive. And frequently, in laboring to make fancy cursive readable, the student wastes valuable time and may not finish.

It would be hard to find an educator who disagrees with the idea that by the time students get to college those who know how to take fast, readable notes in lectures get higher scores on tests than those who don't. Every study guide, college prep handbook, and academic counselor says the same thing: whether it's printing or cursive or a hybrid, good, rapid handwriting is essential.

[1] I'd like to know, too, what kind of cursive it was, and what the scorers would have to say about differences between true cursive, true printing, and the fusion that works for many of us.

But it's also in short supply, and so the first resort of many students is not a notebook but a laptop—a tradeoff that does not always please their professors. Georgetown law prof David Cole banned laptops from his classroom in 2007. As he wrote in a *Wall Street Journal* essay, "Note-taking on a laptop encourages verbatim transcription. The note-taker tends to go into stenographic mode and no longer processes information in a way that is conducive to the give and take of classroom discussion." In addition, now that so many campuses—including classrooms—are wi-fi equipped, "With the aid of Microsoft and Google, we have effectively put at every seat a library of magazines, a television, and the opportunity for real-time side conversations." Multitasking? "I don't buy it," Cole says. "Attention diverted is attention diverted." In a subsequent survey, he found that about 80 percent of his students reported being more engaged in class discussion when they are laptop-free. But their handwriting may present them with its own problem: unreadable notes. Poorly trained handwriters lose legibility as they gain speed.

The fact is that speed is something that should be emphasized from the beginning. Steve Graham told me that second-graders who can write only nine or ten letters per minute (a typical speed for a child having trouble with handwriting) will produce less, will lose their train of thought, will write less coherently and with less planning. Many of the teachers I talked to say those kids will also hate to write—meaning that not only will they hate having to produce handwriting, they'll hate to write *at all*. School compositions, essays, tests, SATs—everything becomes a chore. And it hardly needs to be said that the more writing people do, the better writers they become—and vice versa.

So what would seem to make very good sense is to teach children a pleasantly legible handwriting that would also be fast. Yes, we live in a speeded-up world—but since we still need to write things down, we need to learn to write them quickly.

HANDWRITING PROGRAMS

Since the scripts of Spencer and Palmer were erased from American culture, modern handwriting instruction programs that advertise themselves as "simplified" have been formulated. Charles Paxton Zaner and Elmer Ward Bloser were close contemporaries of Palmer, but their handwriting schools, which also taught engraving, English composition, and other subjects, were not as widespread. Today, the Zaner-Bloser system is the industry leader, along with D'Nealian (devised by Donald Neil Thurber), which are aggressively marketed both to schools and to home schoolers.[2]

But most twentieth-century cursives turn out to be some variation on Pizza Palmer—same basic recipe, slightly different toppings:

Zaner-Bloser

D'Nealian

Then there's "Handwriting Without Tears" (HWT), which jettisons most of the curlicues and eliminates the rightward slant on the theory that children are more comfortable with upright letters because they look more like the print they're already familiar with from books:

Handwriting Without Tears

But does it really make sense for children to turn out writing that resembles what they see in books? And except for its uprightness, how similar is it, really? Also, as Charlemagne's penmanship committee discovered in the ninth century, it seems to be true for nearly all writers that a slight rightward slant ends up being easier, quicker, and kinder to the hand muscles than writing straight up—most people, no matter what method they learn, eventually ease into a slant. In the early 1900s, there was a short-lived fad for teaching vertical script, based on the theory that slanted cursive can cause curvature of the spine and vision problems in children—a theory that was quickly disproved. As Lehman reports in *Handwriting Models for Schools*, an upright hand is actually much more difficult for children to master.[3]

Can we call today's scripts simplified? Well, A. N. Palmer would certainly think so, and Platt Rogers Spencer would probably recommend remedial training for everyone involved. But all these styles retain their share of loops, the unnecessarily convoluted *G* and *S*, the backward *F*, the time-wasting turnarounds on most of the ascenders and descenders (*b*, *f*, *g*, *q*, *y*, etc.), the sailboat *I*, and the double-looped *J*. D'Nealian and HWT even preserve the unrepentant "*Q* like a 2."

The publishers of these systems attempt to make handwriting practice fun, using games, cartoons, finger painting, sidebars, and an occasional touch of wackiness that might have disconcerted Spencer, Palmer, and Sister Victorine, but that, theoretically at least, keep the kids interested. *Fun* seems like an excellent idea, especially when you think of those grim period photographs of rows of students doggedly churning out Palmer exercises. Today, the exercises are still there, in a series of workbooks, complete with dotted lines and repetitive letter-forming, but they're child-friendly, peppered with colorful pictures of animals, birds, and happy kids.

All these handwriting programs have value: a good teacher who presents the instruction in a flexible, non-dogmatic, non-

3 One of its stubborn proponents was Alonzo Reed in his *Word Lessons* (1884). Reed was also one of the inventors of sentence diagramming.

judgmental way—and does manage to make it *fun*—can do enormous good in the classroom.

But as I pondered the handwriting issue, the question came to me in a blinding flash: why teach two different handwritings at all? Why must children be burdened with printing and then, a year or two later, move on to the radically different cursive script, learning a whole new set of letters?

With this in mind, the D'Nealian heart seems to be in the right place. They claim that children learn the script "on a continuum, without a serious break in the development process. eighty-seven percent of [printed] D'Nealian lower case letters are the same as their cursive version. Children easily move into cursive writing when ready."

Well, this may be true, but that other 13 percent seems to consist of those Palmerian squiggles and loops. The more I look at them, the more arbitrary and superfluous they seem, and they simply increase my bewilderment: why shouldn't children learn only one good, plain, solid, simple, easy, basic, legible, attractive—and fast—way of writing, from day one?

ITALIC WRITING

Like most good ideas, mine is not original. Over the years, in pursuit of that goal, there have been several attempts to promote a simplified, everyday version of the Italic script of sixteenth-century masters of the art like Arrighi and Palatino, even for very young children.

In 1899, as Palmermania was getting off the ground, an Englishwoman named Mary Monica Bridges (wife of the poet Robert Bridges), capitalizing on the interest in letter arts popularized by William Morris and the Arts and Crafts revival, published *A New Handwriting for Teachers*, which recommended teaching schoolchildren sixteenth-century Italic. A generation later, in 1929, a study by Arthur I. Gates and Helen Brown in the *Journal of Educational Research* concluded that, perhaps, "by selecting the best elements from cursive and print-scripts, a writing alphabet may be discovered which, by combining the merits of the various existing rivals, will be superior to any one and make the learning of two alphabets unnecessary."

Amazingly, the printing we all learned in school—known also as *manuscript writing*, and often called *ball and stick* from the way the *b*'s, *d*'s, and other letters are formed—has been around for less than a hundred years. Marjorie Wise, another Englishwoman, introduced it to the New York City public schools in the 1920s. Until then, only cursive had been taught, but Wise felt that simple, clear upright printing would be easier for young children.

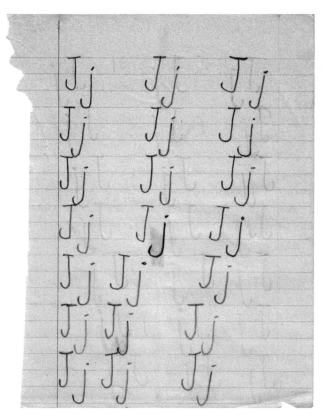

The author's pursuit of the perfect J, grade 1

Very quickly, the traditional pattern took hold: print-script in first grade, cursive in third. Even the Palmer Company endorsed early printing as a worthy overture to their famous Method. However, print-script has always had its detractors. The British educator Alec Hay, in his essay "Handwriting in Schools," commented in the early 1960s, "The writing of single letters, isolated, without joins, gives the young child the idea that the individual letter is the most important shape he is required to make, whereas the whole purpose of this elementary training (parallel with the teaching of reading) is...an understanding and correct transcription of whole words."

Nan Barchowsky developed her Italic handwriting program, known as BFH (Barchowsky Fluent Handwriting), after two decades teaching handwriting in American elementary schools. Barchowsky says that, in print-script, "The characters are drawn slowly, rather than written freely. Rhythm suffers because most print-script models lack the design elements that allow them to flow. Many children confuse the placement of the lines that form letters. Reversals become a problem."

As the Scottish calligrapher, educator, and Italic buff Tom Gourdie wrote in his *Guide to Better Handwriting* (in which he calls print-script "staccato writing—all stop and start"), "As any number of teachers will testify, this is fraught with difficulties and upsets" and produces "calligraphically crippled children."[4]

Even Marjorie Wise eventually repudiated the teaching of printing and became a convert to the notion that children should be taught one beautiful, flowing script—namely, Italic. In 1952, she became a board member of the Society of Italic Handwriting, founded by the calligrapher Alfred Fairbank, himself a great advocate of Italic for children.

In his delightful book *Sweet Roman Hand: Four Hundred Years of Italic Cursive Script* (1952), the Englishman Wilfrid

4 The legendary Tom Gourdie died in 1995 at age ninety-one. In the hospital during his last illness, disturbed by the sloppiness of the name-label attached to his bed, he reportedly began instructing the nurses in the proper way to hold a pen.

Blunt made an eloquent case for its comeback, calling it one of the finest legacies of the Renaissance. Blunt (1901–1987) was the brother of Anthony Blunt, the famous spy who passed British state secrets to the KGB. Wilfrid was rather less colorful. He may even have been a bit stuffy (he considered Monet and Cézanne "pornographic"). But he was an unusual guy: an excellent singer, a passionate gardener, the author of a biography of Linnaeus, and an "out" homosexual in the '30s. He was also mad about fine penmanship. As a senior drawing master at Eton for more than twenty years, he encouraged his students in the use of Italic cursive, and his book is full of remarkable examples of the script by young Etonians he had taught:

> I wondered whether you would be kind enough to send me an example of your handwriting. I am only twelve but am very interested in this subject. you may know my cousin Peter Usborne,

David Usborne, age 12

> Such a great amount as to make any grea to the needs for the church's employment. missionaries who go to minister to the Hea mainly voluntarily, and thus they eviden

Anthony Bedford Russell, age 17

If it had been up to Blunt, this is the kind of script we all would produce every time we wrote a post card or took a note in class.

The movement toward teaching Italic in schools has flowered impressively in the city of Portland, Oregon. Lloyd

Reynolds (1902–1978), an English professor at Reed College there, had, like countless handwriting devotees before him, been enamored of lettering all his life. (As he put it, "The letters would not leave me alone.") He was also a lifelong disciple of "the three Bills: Blake, Morris, and Shakespeare." Reynolds discovered calligraphy in 1934. He studied the work of Fairbank, Johnston, and other masters, immersed himself in the calligraphy of the Arts and Crafts Revival, and resolved to make "the promotion of Italic cursive script" his goal—especially, as he said in an autobiographical note, "after teachers reported that students who mastered the Italic handwriting did better in all of their studies. Having a script that acted as an aid rather than a hindrance made the schoolwork easier and more satisfying."

In *Italic Calligraphy & Handwriting*, Reynolds provides instructions for producing the lively and graceful script for which he was known. His recommendations are sometimes eccentric but refreshingly down-to-earth. When you're practicing, he says, write big: "Smaller writing tends to look better than it is, for details are not clearly seen." To keep a "flower-light touch," you must "watch your forefinger—if it collapses, you are pressing too hard." Above all, "Avoid rote practice. When you become tired or careless, drop it and do something else." He also points out, helpfully, "A letter is mostly untouched paper. There is very little ink on a written or printed page"—so watch the spaces between letters and between lines: the blank areas are as important as the inked ones. He advises working to music—it will "teach you much about the possibilities of rhythm in pen touch and movement"—and finds Mozart's *Symphony No. 40 in G Minor* particularly effective. And he says to try writing with your eyes closed, to see "whether you can trust your hand and wrist." In summary:

Practice critically.

Reynolds branched out at Reed and began teaching a class in calligraphy. He was a charismatic teacher, interested not only in hand-lettering but also in typefaces. Among his students were a number of poets—Gary Snyder, Lew Welch (who, during his brief stint as an adman, supposedly wrote the deathless line "Raid kills bugs dead"), and Philip Whalen, who beautifully hand-lettered his own poetry and journals. Probably the most famous, however, was Steve Jobs, the founder of Apple, Inc. In a commencement address he gave at Stanford in 2005, Jobs recalled that, if he had never taken that course in college,[5] "the Macintosh computer would have never had multiple typefaces or proportionally spaced fonts. And since Windows just copied the Mac, it's likely that no personal computer would have them." Another student, Chuck Bigelow, now a Stanford professor and a type designer, recalled Reynolds's ability to make Italic writing magical: "When you write in an Italic hand," he used to remind his students, "you are making the same kinds of motions that Queen Elizabeth I made when she practiced Chancery Cursive as a teenager..., the same motions as Michelangelo."

Reynolds created a series of twenty half-hour programs on Italic writing for Oregon Educational Television and was Oregon's first (and so far only) Calligrapher Laureate.

Portland became the unofficial Italic Handwriting Capital of the U.S. Reynolds's passion for letters was in the air, like the mist off the river. In 1979, two handwriting teachers there, Barbara Getty and Inga Dubay, got together and devised a rapid, streamlined Italic script—a simplified Renaissance-influenced style that's a hybrid of printing and cursive:

5 Actually, Jobs dropped out of Reed after six months, but he hung around for another year or so taking courses that appealed to him.

Lloyd Reynolds's Mercedes

Aa Bb Cc Dd Ee Ff Gg Hh Ii Jj Kk Ll Mm Nn Oo Pp Qq Rr Ss Tt Uu Vv Ww Xx Yy Zz

Teaching traditional cursive to third-graders, Getty had seen it go badly. Boys, in particular, she says, felt silly executing all the Palmerish curlicues, but in fact none of the children took to it easily. And she observes that, even if it is mastered in school, cursive doesn't hold up well in later life: America is a "please print" nation because most people's cursive is illegible, or close to it. At best, many letters are ambiguous, easy to mess up when you're in a hurry:

mirror   aluminum   remember

Working with Portland State University, the two women published a series of lucid and attractive books—the Getty-Dubay Italic Handwriting Series—designed for teaching their handwriting to schoolchildren from kindergarten to sixth grade. Intended as an alternative to "looped cursive," their term for any standard cursive program, the Getty-Dubay system is loop-and-curl-free, and it joins letters only where joining them seems sensible and comfortable.

Both Getty and Dubay had been students of Lloyd Reynolds, and both are accomplished calligraphers; their books were initially handwritten by the two of them—an appealing gimmick that helped to popularize the system:

WRITING TOOLS

MONOLINE TOOLS (pp. 13–60) No. 2 pencil, medium or fine fiber tip pen, ballpoint, cartridge ink pen or fountain pen may be used to complete pp. 14–50. The line written with a monoline tool is of a constant thickness like this writing.

EDGED PENS (pp. 61–74.)

These three lines are written with an edged pen.

PENCIL/PEN POSITION

Hold your monoline instrument or edged pen with your thumb and index finger, resting it on your middle finger. Rest the shaft of the writing instrument near the large knuckle.

To relax hand, tap index finger on writing instrument three times. Repeat as needed.

Getty-Dubay has been used in the Portland Public Schools for twenty-four years. A Portland teacher and Italic fan, Deziré Clarke, comments that learning Italic gives her third- and fourth-graders "the opportunity to slow down in this computer/video game world," and that their final product "shines with excellence." It has been adopted by other public schools, as well as private and charter schools, and is used widely among home schoolers in the United States and in Canada, valued not only because it teaches clear, simple handwriting but because, as *Time* magazine put it in a 1983 article, Getty-Dubay demonstrates that "the teaching of proper handwriting evokes children's innate sense of visual order and beauty. It gives children an eye for good design."

Obviously, children aren't the only ones who can be taught to write legibly and like it. Getty and Dubay have also put together a book for adults, called *Write Now*, which is especially popular among doctors[6] and businessmen—and among computer technicians, who find an immersion in beautiful handwriting a breath of fresh air, a welcome respite from the mechanical cyberworld.

6 One of whom coined the word "loopectomy" to describe what their course did to his writing.

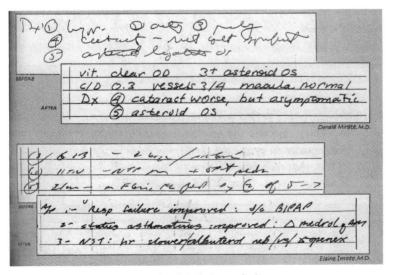

Doctors' scripts, before and after

It will come as no surprise to anyone that physicians are prime customers for handwriting therapy. Medical cacography has become a staple of popular culture. The TV drama *Grey's Anatomy* often tackles the issue: in one 2007 episode, Dr. Izzie Stevens tells the interns she's supervising, "Penmanship saves lives! Is that a 7, or is that a 9? If I have to ask myself that in the middle of an emergency, your patient is dead. You killed him. With your handwriting. Think about that!" In a 2007 episode of *Curb Your Enthusiasm*, Larry David is dating a doctor who writes him an illegible mash note; the joke is that he has to take it to a pharmacist to decipher.

But none of this means that handwriting is no longer useful. As *Newsweek* pointed out in a 2007 article, "Predictions of handwriting's demise didn't begin with the computer; they date back to the introduction of the Remington typewriter in 1873....No one has suggested that the invention of the calculator means we don't have to teach kids how to add, and spelling is still a prized skill in the era of spell check." Kate Gladstone, a professional "handwriting repairwoman" in Albany, New York, has worked with doctors[7] at hospitals all over the country that have, out of desperation, brought her in to help their medical staff get the hang of handwriting. (Attending such a course provides Continuing Medical Education credits, under the "patient safety" umbrella.) The conventional wisdom, of course, is that doctors produce more slovenly scribbles than members of any other profession. Medication errors, it is said, result in thousands of deaths annually. It's uncertain how many are caused by illegible handwriting, but in 1999 a cardiologist was fined $225,000 by a jury in Texas because a prescription he had written for Isordil, a drug for heart pain, was misread by the pharmacist as Plendil, used for high blood pressure. The patient died.[8] The pharmacist who filled the prescription was fined an equal amount. Medical regulations require a pharmacist to check with the physician if there is any question regarding a prescription.

7 Her PowerPoint presentation begins with a pen dripping blood and the caption, "The most deadly medical instrument." As she says, "It gets their attention."

8 The Florida Healthcare Coalition distributes bumper stickers and buttons with the slogan I WON'T ACCEPT A PRESCRIPTION IF I CAN'T READ THE WRITING.

It's not just doctors. Nearly everyone writes badly: dentists, nurses, poets, psychiatrists, hairdressers, zookeepers, chemists, schoolteachers, electricians. You name it. When we put pen to paper, most of us—especially those born too late to have had Palmer Method whaled into them at an impressionable age—squeeze out hideous and barely legible scribbles, and the handwriting even of some Palmer Methodists has deteriorated with age, lack of use, endless keyboarding, and the rigors of multitasking.

Kate Gladstone is also an advocate of Italic writing and, according to her, no adult is too far gone to learn it. She offers to wreak dramatic improvements in the script of anyone who will send her a sample and pay her fee—no matter what their age. (She points out that plenty of monks in the Middle Ages started out as "illiterate fifteen-year-olds" who had to be trained to write.) Gladstone is horrified that her service is necessary, that schools haven't ensured that all students can produce a neat hand by the time they graduate, and that the handwriting of some teachers—themselves the products of years of no handwriting instruction in schools—is sometimes so bad that the kids can't read it. The Steve Graham study I cited earlier found that, while 81 percent of schools include some kind of handwriting instruction in the first three grades, only 12 percent of teachers feel that the education courses they took in college prepared them for the task of teaching it.

"If people who can't count were found to be teaching math," Gladstone says, "there'd be a report on *60 Minutes*, it would be on the cover of *Time*, and there would be several congressional investigations." As it is, "Nobody says boo." She's also indignant that children must learn ball-and-stick printing for a year or two, and then switch to the radically different cursive most schools teach: "We'd call it ridiculous to try to teach math entirely in Roman numerals up to second or third grade, then suddenly drop it all and start over again with modern Arabic numerals."

9 Reasonably coherent abecedarian sentences using all twenty-six letters of the alphabet. The most common is *The quick brown fox jumps over the lazy dog*.

I sent Kate Gladstone my own increasingly awful scrawl, providing the alphabets, casual samples, and pangrams[9] she requested:

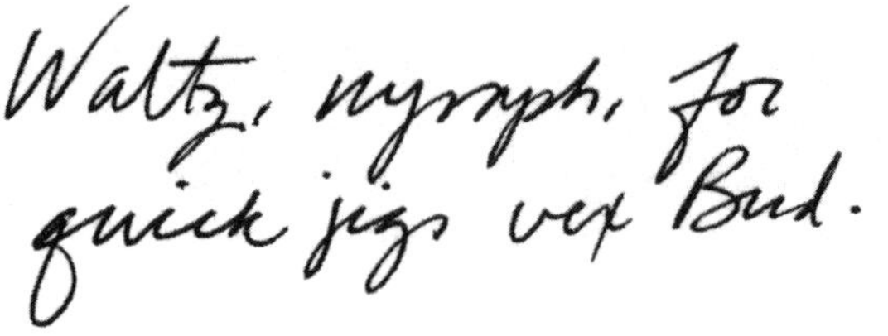

Waltz, nymph, for
quick jigs vex Bud.

She emailed me six pages of suggestions, along with some handy visuals.

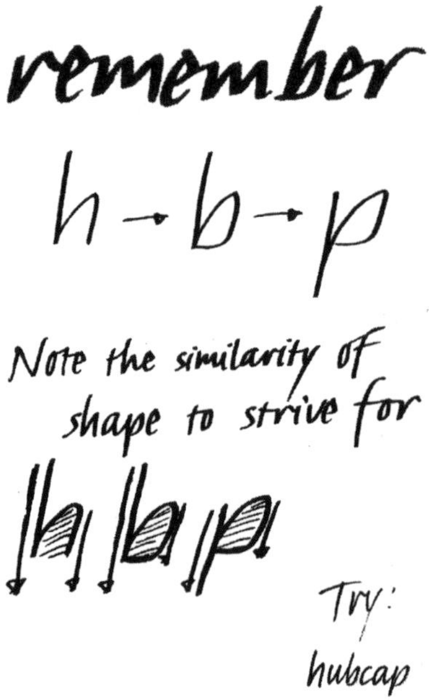

remember
h - b - p
Note the similarity of
shape to strive for
Try:
hubcap

She allowed as how my slant is good, my lower-case *h* isn't bad, and my numerals are passable. Except for a caution to "keep away from conventional cursive forms" when I write capitals, her suggestions were for lower-case fix-ups only, since they comprise 98 percent of our writing.

Otherwise—well, as I said, it was six pages' worth of ideas. Single-spaced.

I printed it out, grabbed my copy of Getty-Dubay's *Write Now*, sat down for an hour with some paper and my favorite gel pen—and watched my handwriting begin a metamorphosis from embarrassingly clumsy to terminally cool.

Some of Gladstone's suggestions were simple, some a bit more challenging, and they were slow to execute until I got used to them. I particularly liked her proposal that I make my lower-case *t* smaller and cross it lower. As she put it, "If you can accustom yourself to making the *t*-bar at the height of the shortest lower-case letters—and also making the *t* less tall than, say, an *l* or an *h*, so that it doesn't look top-heavy with the bar placed at the short-letter height—you will find that words containing both a *t* and some tall letters suddenly become much easier to read."

Tied   versus   *tied*

She also had some very good tips for making a prettier and more legible lower-case *e*. Nearly everyone could profit from this: *e* is the most used and the most-often indecipherable letter in the alphabet. "A quick fix that has helped many," Gladstone says, "is simply not to attach any letter onto the *e*—write the *e*, then lift the pen and start over." For me, the most important thing to remember was to start the e with a straight line pointing up in a northeast direction, then curve back in a C shape:

—making sure it's open enough to show clearly that this is indeed an *e* and not an *r* or part of a *u* or an undotted *i*.

before   *after*

Better yet, learn to write the "Renaissance two-stroke e"—
basically a hook and a comma:

$$ \angle\ +\ ? \ =\ \ell $$

It's a very handsome *e*, but I find it slow and difficult to write,
and the results I get are clunky. I'm practicing—the *e* of
Michelangelo is worth striving for!—but I fear I'm going to end
up a one-stroke *e* kind of person, which is sort of like someone
who can only drive automatic shift, or who buys pre-chopped
garlic in a jar.

My lower-case *k* is a happier story. Gladstone showed me
how to construct it from an *h*: start to make an h, but stop as
you reach its humped back and add a graceful downstroke:

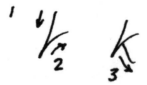

It's a lovely way of doing it, and it works, but it's hard to get
used to because, in an unconscious throwback to a sixth-cen-
tury Uncial script, I've been making little *k*'s like sloppy,
smaller spinoffs of my vaguely Palmerish big *K*'s most of my
writing life:

You can see my hesitant beginnings of reform in *beekeeper*. I still have a long road to travel.

As I combined Gladstone's personalized instruction with some of the ideas in the Getty-Dubay books, my writing, unexpectedly, began to look like a looser and less constipated version of the pretentious, arty script I used in college. I remember how hard I had to concentrate to produce it, especially taking notes in class, aware of the fact that my friends and I often traded notes when we studied for exams. Twit that I was, I was writing to impress. All these years later, what I want is ease and freedom, and that's what my handwriting practice began to give me.

I found the all-time best Getty-Dubay tip was to avoid what they call "scoop and loop," the overly rounded connectors that can lend to many people's handwriting—mine, at least—a disagreeably girlish look that almost cries out for those dopey little circles dotting the *i*'s:

scooping and looping

Instead, I've been trying to use a straight diagonal line when joining letters—not a U-shape but something closer to an angle:

no scooping, no looping

This may seem trivial, but the neat and pointy results in my own script impressed me so much that I called Barbara Getty to thank her. She told me she and Inga stole it directly from Arrighi. Which brings us back to dear old Wilfrid Blunt, who put it like this: "I have often been asked why we should turn to sixteenth-century Italy for our pattern. I can only reply: where else can we find a better, or even an adequate, model?"

Once I started writing in Italic, I found it impossible to disagree. The result of my tinkering is an enormous improvement in my handwriting.

Very rapid notetaking

Sometimes my script still looks rushed, or uneven—a good sense of proportion eludes me (I do much better when writing on lined paper). And, so far, it lacks character—maybe, with time, the blandness will pass. But it's way more readable, just as quick as my old scribble, nicer to look at, and historically interesting.

PEACEFUL COEXISTENCE

All the handwriting programs I investigated have merit, but no matter how easy one system may be or how legible another, no matter whether children think it's a lark or a grind, no matter how determinedly it's marketed, and no matter how evident it is that fast, clear handwriting leads to future success, fewer and fewer schools, unfortunately, are teaching it in any form whatsoever beyond the third grade. Because what really excites trendy, up-to-date educators is the idea that the computer ends the problem of bad handwriting—that *key-boarding* is what everyone needs to learn, not how to push a pen across paper.

Why is it *keyboarding*? What happened to *typing*? The noun *keyboard* used as a verb dates back to 1961—the days when key-punching became a career. Keypunch operators loaded "punch cards" (almost always called "IBM cards," though there were other manufacturers) with data by punching holes—using a keyboard—at strategic places that made sense to the early com-puters that would "read" the cards. Today *keyboard* is used more often as a participle—*keyboarding*—than as a direct "action verb." There are few people who could say "Keyboard this asap!" or "I need to keyboard up my notes" with a straight face.

Like so many words in the great bubbling stew of the Eng-lish language, *keyboarding* is irrational—we don't say *pianoing* when we pound the ivories—but the word *typing* wears the aura of the days when the feminist movement cautioned women not to learn to type or they'd never advance out of the steno pool. Machines of the time may have been less user-friendly, but people were, of necessity, more intimate with them: a typewriter needed paper fed into it, the carriage return lever manipulated, the platen adjusted for line spacing, the ribbon replaced as needed, the keys unstuck when they jammed. The keyboard on a computer, however, is the only part of the com-puter we really interact with. The computer can crash, hang, freeze, become corrupted, or perform illegal operations, but the keyboard is an entity in itself, with its own separate func-tioning, and it merits its own verb. Condensing *typing on a keyboard* to just plain *keyboarding* has a high-tech ring to it, a pleasantly up-to-date crispness.

But, usage questions aside, which should children learn? To type on a keyboard or to write with a pen on paper?

The issue brings to mind an Isaac Asimov story, "The Feeling of Power," in which, in some future world completely controlled by machines, a lowly technician comes up with the radical idea of "computing without a computer." He laboriously copies numbers from his super-calculator onto a piece of paper with an "artist's stylus" and, before a puzzled, skeptical committee, multiplies them, in "an imitation of the workings of the computer." This wacko idea—termed *graphitics*, "from the old European word *grapho*, meaning *to write"*— slowly catches on, and the powers-that-be begin to envision a world of limitless possibility, a world "liberated from the machine." Asimov's satirical point, of course, is that technology can become too powerful, at the expense of the mental activity that makes us human.[10] The story is a favorite of college math teachers, one of whom writes, "Once the holy numbers pop up on the screen, it's hard to convince people to use their brains."

Only the most pious Luddite could argue against the idea that learning to use a computer is an essential skill children should be taught. As far back as 1935, the Illinois Board of Education was recommending the teaching of typing in elementary school. The current thinking is that children begin serious keyboarding instruction in third grade, when they have the proper eye-hand coordination and language skills and before they've developed too many bad keyboard habits fooling around on the computer at home.

Like it or not, most of those kids will probably be earning their living tapping a keyboard someday, somehow, somewhere. There aren't many jobs that don't require a measure of computer competence.[11] Nor should the growing use of the computer for plain old fun be ignored. The Children's Digital Media Center (CDMC), a five-university consortium based at Georgetown, studies children's computer and Internet use and how it affects them long-term. In their most recent report (2005), the CDMC found that twelve- to fifteen-year-old California students spend more than 90 minutes a day instant

10 His other, subtler point is the ruthless grab for power by those who have it and want more. At the end of the story, Aub, the technician, discovers that the military plans to replace computerized missiles with manned ones because "a man is much more dispensable than a computer." Aub kills himself because he "can't face the responsibility involved in having invented graphitics."

11 Or cell phone keyboard competence: in Japan, there's a fad for writing novels on cell phone screens. You use your thumb to tap the keys while holding the phone steady with your little finger. While writing her eighth novel, a twenty-two-year-old named Satomi Nakamura broke a blood vessel on her right pinkie. She says, "PCs might be easier to type on, but I've had a cell phone since I was in sixth grade, so it's easier for me to use."

messaging friends, 31.4 minutes sampling and downloading music, and 22 minutes sending and reading e-mail. Surely, these numbers will only increase, and if kids are going to sit at the computer pecking away, they should be pecking efficiently. In the words of a customer in the computer store near my house where I had my laptop overhauled, "Computers ain't going nowheres."[12] Or, as Leigh E. Zeitz, a professor of Instructional Technology at the University of Northern Iowa, puts it, "Today's world requires us to be efficient keyboarders to interact and communicate with others through technology."

Zeitz has taught students at all levels, from elementary school to graduate school, and has been involved in the field of education technology for twenty-eight years. It's his opinion that what he calls "the world of word processing" is changing the way we think about writing. For him, the most important computer-era change in student writing is that much of it is produced for publication. Students in the classroom are sitting at keyboards creating books, anthologies, blogs, wikis. Their work is not written on paper, submitted to a teacher, graded, and put away somewhere. It is going to be seen—or at least *can* be seen—not only by a teacher but by whoever chooses to look at it: parents, friends, peers, and, increasingly, anyone with Internet access. For these students, it's not just their grades but their reputations that are on the line. "This adds to the perceived value of the writing," Zeitz says. "It gets into their blood and makes them want to be better writers."

He admits that his own handwriting is wretched; he learned to type in tenth grade, and is far more comfortable on the keyboard than behind the pen, which he associates with "drudgery and fear." He especially loves the ease of revision on a computer. "When I don't have to worry about mistakes," he told me, "the ideas flow out of my fingers." In an amusing reversal of the usual process, Zeitz once composed a love letter to his wife on the keyboard, revised it to his satisfaction, then care-

12 He didn't say this happily: his computer had just crashed for the second time, destroying everything on his hard drive. My laptop had slowed to a crawl because it had more viruses than an influenza research lab. I'm tempted to write "Q.E.D.," but I will refrain.

fully copied it by hand onto paper. "Students can't handwrite now because they *don't* handwrite," he says, "and they don't because they don't want to." Instead, they become keyboarding whiz-kids.

His opinion is borne out by—of all people—Nabeel Khaliq, the Canadian sixth-grader who won first prize in his age category in the 2002 World Handwriting Contest, sponsored by the Handwriting for Humanity club. In interviews, Nabeel said that he loves handwriting and is proud of his glorious script (he comes from a family of accomplished cursive writers), but for his extensive correspondence with his cousins in Pakistan, he admitted: "I'd rather do it on the computer."

But everyone doesn't feel that way—not only middle-aged pen nuts but students themselves. Teachers who do teach cursive routinely talk about the pride their students take in perfecting it, and many students who are deeply into keyboarding retain a preference for the act of handwriting. Even Leigh Zeitz the keyboarding maven respects what handwriting can offer, and doesn't think it should be taken out of the curriculum.

I discussed all this with Kate Olson, a teacher at Longfellow Middle School in La Crosse, Wisconsin, which houses a charter school called School of Technology and the Arts (SOTA). As one tool for engaging her students, Olson has set up a blog where they can practice writing and reading skills incorporating twenty-first-century technology. The blog is open for comments from anyone. When Olson used this forum to ask her SOTA sixth-graders, who were being introduced to keyboarding, whether they preferred typing or handwriting, some noted that once their skills improve they might start to prefer typing, but, by about four to one, they would rather handwrite. The reasons they gave ranged from "When you're writing, your hands aren't all over the place like when you're typing" and "You don't type a thank you letter, I don't know if it is more sincere but you just don't," to what lies nearer the heart of the matter: "I think that writing is actually more important. It is really hard to believe how many people don't have computers at home." Kate Olson expanded on this: several of her students, she told me, don't have easy access to computers outside of school, and "a lot of them" have access restricted by their parents for various reasons.

The truth is that millions of children are sent out into the world armed with lousy handwriting, great keyboarding skills—and no computer. The admirable nonprofit organization called One Laptop per Child (OLPC) aims to provide children in developing countries with an innovative cheap, child-size laptop called the XO, to help them become better educated and, in the process, lift themselves out of poverty. There is as yet no comparable American program. In a study conducted for the Leadership Conference on Civil Rights in 2005, Dr. Robert W. Fairlie of the University of California at Santa Cruz reported that only half of black and Latino households are likely to have a computer on the premises, compared with about 75 percent of whites. More than twenty million American children (26 percent) have no computer access at home.

These figures will no doubt change as computers become as ubiquitous as once-exotic items like phones and televisions—although, as Fairlie notes in a subsequent study (2007), "The 'digital divide' is large and does not appear to be disappearing soon." Furthermore, as Kate Gladstone puts it, "Until someone makes a computer that needs no batteries or electricity; that works after being stepped on, chewed, or dropped in a toilet; and that's cheap enough to sell in packs or give in multiples to school children, the humble pen and pencil—and the need for legible handwriting—will remain alive." She points out that, post-Katrina, some parts of the affected area were without electricity for long periods of time, and local hospitals, in addition to lighting operating rooms with flashlights, had to resort to actual pens and paper for keeping records—records that ended up being largely unreadable. She also told me an amusing (sort of) story about checking into a hotel in an area suffering under a prolonged power outage. The staff suddenly had to hand-write the names of guests, addresses, credit card numbers—and the only employee with handwriting anyone could read was a man on the verge of retirement. If it had happened a few months later, there would have been no one left who could write a decent hand.

* * * *

As a writer, I am heavily dependent on the notebook I carry in my pocket when I leave for my daily walk. I wish I could say that the ideas that come to me as I cover my three miles are permanently stored in my memory, but alas—brilliant though they may be, if I don't jot them down, they're gone. My friend Bill Stanton is a New York City photographer whose books often involve his rambling around town taking preliminary notes. At home, he's a Photoshop whiz and general computer master—in the field, he's obsessively dependent on his notebooks: [13]

13 "To lose a passport was the least of one's worries; to lose a notebook was a catastrophe." —Bruce Chatwin in *The Songlines*

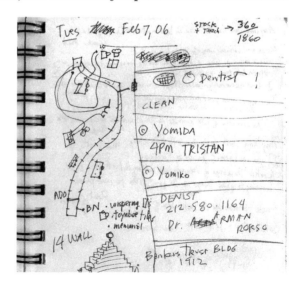

Travelers on the move, scientists in the field, birdwatchers recording the details on wing bars and beaks, hikers inspired to write a poem on a mountaintop, Peace Corps volunteers, workers in deserts, jungles, rainforests, inner cities, disaster areas—many of them will not have access to computers.

There are less exotic computer-free zones. In the small country town where until recently I spent summers, I was called as a witness at a hearing at the local courthouse. The judge, the D.A., the clerk, and all the lawyers took notes by hand—not a computer in sight.

As time goes by, our dwindling natural resources may force us to depend on computers less, rather than more. According to a report from the U.S. Government's Energy Information Administration, the demand for electricity to power home electronics (especially color TVs and computer equipment) is expected to grow significantly over the next two decades: "EIA projects electricity consumption to grow 3.5 percent annually for color TVs and computer equipment through 2025, to more than double the level of consumption in 2003." As fossil fuels (which some power plants use to generate electricity) become scarcer and more costly, it seems inevitable that, even leaving aside apocalyptic worst-case scenarios, unless we become committed to generating power from solar panels and wind turbines, electricity may have to be rationed. California came close to this during their electricity crisis of 2000–2001 with its rolling blackouts—and we in the Northeast have vivid memories of the 2003 blackout, caused by a glitch in an Ohio branch of the country's vast (and often archaic) electrical grid system. Computer manufacturers are reportedly "working on" the problem of becoming greener but, in general, energy use isn't something keyboard enthusiasts talk much about.[14]

If we lived in an ideal world, no one would write illegibly, and no one would have to hunt and peck when faced with a keyboard, either. The dual skills of handwriting and typing

14 Nor is the rampant carpal tunnel syndrome that may well afflict future generations. If *The Graduate* were being filmed today, the businessman who takes young Dustin Hoffman aside to offer a bit of career advice might put it differently. Instead of "I want to say just one word to you: plastics," it would be two words: "hand surgery."

are both ways of putting words on paper—of setting down our thoughts and ideas, of communicating with others. Both methods have value. The important element is fluency, whether on the keyboard or with the pen. Either way, the act of writing needs to become automatic, freeing up our brains for what they're best at: thinking.

Why can't the keyboard and the pen lie down together like the lion and the lamb and live in harmony? This is not a rhetorical question. I sincerely wish some influential educator, or a politician looking for the mom-and-pop vote, or PTA groups who really care about their children's futures, would face up to the importance of handwriting and find a way for our overstressed schools to teach their over-tested students to be literate citizens of the twenty-first century who can wield both a pencil and a mouse with ease, with skill, with pride—and with pleasure.

Bibliography

BOOKS

Paul Auster, *The Story of My Typewriter* (Distributed Art Publishers, Inc., 2002)

Camillo Baldi, *A Method to Recognize the Nature and Quality of a Writer from His Letters* (1622), translated by Robert Backman in *Camillo Baldi, His Life and Works* (Handwriting Analysis Research Library)

George Bickham, *The Universal Penman* (Dover Publications, Inc., 1941)

Wilfrid Blunt, *Sweet Roman Hand* (London: James Barrie, 1952)

Milton N. Bunker, *What Handwriting Tells You About Yourself, Your Friends, and Famous People* (Nelson-Hall, 1965)

Milton N. Bunker, *Handwriting Analysis: the Art and Science of Reading Character by Grapho-Analysis* (Nelson-Hall, 1972)

Mary Monica Waterhouse Bridges, *A New Handwriting for Teachers* (Oxford University Press, 1899)

June Downey, *Graphology & the Psychology of Handwriting* (Baltimore: Warwick & York, 1919)

Marc Drogin, *Medieval Calligraphy* (Dover Publications, Inc., 1980)

Barbara Getty & Inga Dubay, *Write Now* (Portland State University, 1991)

Tom Gourdie, *A Guide to Better Handwriting* (Viking, 1967)

William E. Henning, *An Elegant Hand: The Golden Age of American Penmanship and Calligraphy*; edited by Paul Melzer (New Castle, DE: Oak Knoll Press, 2006)

Donald Jackson, *The Story of Writing* (Taplinger Publishing Co., 1981)

Charles L. Lehman, *Handwriting Models for Schools* (Portland, OR; Alcuin Press, 1976)

F. G. Netherclift, *The Handbook to Autographs* (London: 1862)

A. S. Osley, editor, *Calligraphy and Paleography: Essays Presented to Alfred Fairbank on his 70th Birthday* (London: Faber & Faber, 1965)

A. S. Osley, editor, *Scribes and Sources: Handbook of the Chancery Hand in the Sixteenth Century: Texts from the Writing-Masters* (Boston: David Godine, 1980)

A. N. Palmer, *The Palmer Method of Business Writing* by A.N. Palmer, 1901, A.N. Palmer Company, New York

Henry Petroski, *The Pencil: A History of Design and Circumstance* (Knopf, 1990)

Tamara Plakins Thornton, *Handwriting in America* (Yale, 1996)

Lloyd J. Reynolds, *Italic Calligraphy and Handwriting: Exercises and Text* (Taplinger Publishing Co, 1976)

Louise Rice, *Character Reading from Handwriting* (Van Nuys, CA: Newcastle Publishing Co., Inc., 1996)

Platt Rogers Spencer, *Theory of the Spencerian System of Practical Penmanship*, 1874, Ivison, Blakeman, Taylor & Co.

Michael Sull, *Learning to Write Spencerian Script; Spencerian Script and Ornamental Penmanship* (Mission, KS: The Lettering Design Group, 1989)

Bernard Wolpe, ed., *A Neue Booke of Copies, 1574* (facsimile) (Oxford University Press, 1962)

WEBSITES

www.analyzemy handwriting.com

www.bantjes.com

www.bfhhandwriting.com

www.dnealian.com

www.handwriting analysisresearchlibrary.org

www.handwriting success.com

www.handwriting thatworks.com

www.hwtears.com

www.iampeth.com

www.leighzeitz.com

www.omniglot.com

www.penworld.com

www.richardspens.com

www.spencerian.com

www.writealetter.org

www.zanerian.com

Image Credits

ALL IMAGES ARE THE
AUTHOR'S EXCEPT
FOR THE FOLLOWING:

p 21 Saleslady photograph
courtesy the Library of
Congress

pp 23 Stylus, 85 handwriting
courtesy Ron Savage

pp 26 Roman Square
Capital, 27 Roman Rustic,
29 Half Uncial, 30 Insular
Miniscule, 34 Carolingian
Minuscule, 120 Elizabeth
I signature, 138 Thoreau
lettering courtesy Margaret
Soucy

pp 26 Woman with stylus,
52 Laszlo Biro photograph
courtesy Wikipedia

pp 29 Monastery
scriptorium, 127 Dickens
manuscript used with
permission from The
Pierpont Morgan Library /
Art Resource, NY

p 33 Swan painting,
courtesy Turi MacCombie

p 35 Gothic joke from
Medieval Calligraphy by
Marc Drogin, reprinted with
permission from Dover
Publications, Inc.

pp 40 Chancery hand, 41
English Roundhand, 43
Arabick, 43 Syriack, 43
putti, 44 bill of sale from
The Universal Penman by
George Bickham, reprinted
with permission from
Dover Publications, Inc.

p 46 Ben Franklin
handwriting courtesy
of Archives & Special
Collections, Franklin
& Marshall University,
Lancaster, PA

pp 49 Parker Pen, 51
Snorkel pen, 149 Esterbrook
pen, 150 Parker 75 pen,
photographs © Richard F.
Binder

p 57 Derwent Pencil
Factory photograph used
with permission from
the Cumberland Pencil
Museum

p 59 Thoreau Pencil
box image used with
permission from the
Thoreau Institute at Walden
Woods

p 60 graphite quill
photograph courtesy
Agelio Batle

pp 62 Spencerian alphabet,
148 Spencerian workshop
image, 71 Spencer
memorial photo courtesy
Michael Sull

pp 63 Spencer portrait, 77
A. N. Palmer portrait, 79
Western Penman, from
*An Elegant Hand: The
Golden Age of American
Penmanship and Calligraphy*
by William E. Henning,
reprinted with permission
from Oak Knoll Press

p 65 Persis Duty Spencer,
1860, by Junius R. Sloan
courtesy Brauer
Museum of Art

p 66 copybook pages
courtesy Patricia Maxson

pp 68 "Kind Words" by
Francis Courtney, 84
Copperplate alphabets
courtesy Nick D'Aquanno

pp 69 Spencer "principles,"
69 capital E, 70 lower-
case K, 70 "whole arm"
image from *Theory of
the Spencerian System of
Practical Penmanship*

pp 72 letter, 73 "little red
book," courtesy Mary Alice
Kier

p 74 Spencerian monoline
courtesy Maureen Vickery,
PenDance Calligraphy &
Engraving

p 74 Saks advertising image
courtesy Marian Bantjes

p 75 Coca-Cola image
courtesy The Coca-Cola
Company. The world
famous Coca-Cola and
Coca-Cola Script Logo
trademarks are registered
trademarks of the Coca-
Cola Company.

pp 80 bedspring ovals, 81
drills, 82 youth with pen,
83 diagram, 83 classroom
students, 76 Palmer
alphabet from *The Palmer
Method of Business Writing*

p 89 writing sample
courtesy Rosamond Cerio
Bennati

pp 90 news photo, 91
writing sample courtesy
Eileen Lawton Oliva

p 96 Michon image
courtesy Handwriting
Analysis Research Library

p 98 Poe signature and
image courtesy The
Edgar Allan Poe Society
of Baltimore

pp 99–100 Bryant,
Emerson, Longellow, Lowell
handwriting samples from
"On Autography"
by Edgar Allan Poe

pp 102 Roy Gardner script,
101 Bunker photo from
*Handwriting Analysis: The
Art and Science of Reading
Character* by Milton N.
Bunker

p 107 June Etta Downey
photo used with
permission from the
American Heritage Center,
University of Wyoming,
June Etta Downey Photo
File negative #16254

p 109 Gordon Allport photo
courtesy Richard I. Evans,
PhD

p 109 Philip K. Vernon
photo courtesy Tony Vernon

pp 112 Mad Bomber image
courtesy Peter Stackpole/
Time & Life Pictures/Getty
Images, 130 Anne Frank
diary courtesy Anne Frank-
Fonds – Basel/Hulton
Archive / Getty Images

p 124 LongPen™ photo
courtesy Matthew Gibson

p 126 Sarah Orne Jewett manuscript used with permission from Houghton Library, Harvard University, MS Am 1743.17 (6)

p 136 Calligraphy invitation envelope courtesy Barbara Getty

p 137 Steinberg poster, exhibition at the Galerie Maeght, Paris, 1966 © The Saul Steinberg Foundation / Artists Rights Society (ARS), New York; photograph by Jack DeAngelis

p 140 *Under Milk Wood* excerpt courtesy Sheila Waters

p 141 Runtrikha script courtesy David Govan

p 141 Vine script courtesy Marshall Wildey

p 142 Byron graffito photograph courtesy Ted Reinert

pp 144 Graffiti image, 184 notebook page courtesy Bill Stanton

p 146 IAMPETH certificate courtesy Rosemary Buczek

p 149 photograph used with permission from Sara Kane

p 150 Winter 2005 Pennant cover, photography by David Bloch; layout by Dede Rekopf and Fran Conn; design, objects, and image courtesy L. Michael Fultz

p 156 Duke of Wellington letter from *The Handbook to Autographs* by F. G. Netherclift (London, 1862)

p 159 handwriting sample courtesy Katherine Florey

pp 162 Zaner Bloser, 162 D'Nealian, 162 Handwriting Without Tears alphabets from Educational Fontware

pp 169 Getty Dubay alphabet, 170 handwritten page, 171 reformed script from *Write Now* by Barbara Getty and Inga Dubay, used with permission

p 167 David Usborne, Anthony Bedford Russell handwriting samples from *Sweet Roman Hand* by Wilfrid Blunt

p 168 "Practice Critically" from *Italic Calligraphy & Handwriting* by Lloyd J. Reynolds, reprinted with permission from Taplinger Publishing Co., Inc.

p 169 Lloyd Reynolds's Mercedes photo courtesy Lloyd Reynolds Papers, Special Collections, Eric V. Hanser Library, Reed College, Portland, Oregon

p 174 "Remember," etc. courtesy Kate Gladstone

Acknowledgements

For sharing their insights, pouring out advice, directing me to sources, helping with research, providing materials, serving as guinea pigs, lending moral support, and generally making this book possible, my deep gratitude[1] goes to:

Rosamond Cerio Bennati

Michelle Bisson

Katherine Florey

Sara Kane

Mary Alice Kier

Becky Kraemer

Turi and Bruce MacCombie

Rich and Pat Maxson

Norma Fox and Harry Mazer

Stuart Miner

Eileen Lawton Oliva

Carl Rubino

Lorelei Russ

Ron Savage

Jane Schwartz

Laura and Leslie Smith

Bill Stanton

[1] The fact that these thank-yous were not written with a fountain pen on monogrammed paper and sent individually by mail does not make them any less heartfelt.